Table of Contents *(cont.)*

Chapter 1
Being a Professional Substitute Teacher

Introduction

Welcome to the profession. Anyone who has ever substitute taught knows that it can be both rewarding and challenging. Many times the substitute teacher is considered successful if he or she is able to simply keep control of a class. Surely, every substitute teacher strives to do much better than that.

The book in your hands was written because so little is available to people in your position. This first chapter is designed to make the experience more meaningful and successful for you and the students. Perhaps you are wondering how you can prepare for a day of substituting for the regular classroom teacher. To address this need, this part of the book is divided into four different categories:

1. At Home
2. When You Arrive at the School
3. Moving Through the Day
4. Before You Leave the School

General Tips

First, though, here are some general tips to help you to smoothly assimilate into your new environment:

- If you want to substitute teach at a particular school, get to know the secretary there. It is often her job to arrange for substitute teachers. Even if she doesn't have to arrange for a replacement teacher, she is frequently asked for suggestions.

- If you want to do long-term subbing, make that known to the school office and to the teachers you sub for. When you talk to them, provide each school with a copy of your résumé.

- Say "yes" as often as possible. When you will be out of town or on vacation, call the person who is responsible for securing subs. Make sure he or she knows when you will return and call him or her as soon as you do.

- If you don't want to work on a particular day, let the person in charge know in advance. If you answer and say "no" too often, you'll stop getting calls.

- Keep a file on each school where you sub. Include administrators' names, a map of the school, a list of faculty, and a copy of the school's rules and procedures. Keep notes about individual teachers and classes. Indicate class rules and routines, whether the teacher leaves a sub folder and lesson plans, what classroom expectations are, how the class behaved, and so on. Keep copies of all your teacher reports.

- Proper preparation for substitute teaching is essential. Your arrival time at the school can be essential to the smooth functioning of your classroom. Taking the correct materials into the classroom can mean an extra five minutes added to your teaching time with the students because you don't need to spend that time looking for essential teaching supplies.

Editor
Eric Migliaccio

Managing Editor
Ina Massler Levin, M.A.

Illustrator
Sue Fullam

Cover Artist
Barb Lorseyedi

Art Manager
Kevin Barnes

Art Director
CJae Froshay

Imaging
Rosa C. See

Publisher
Mary D. Smith, M.S. Ed.

Super Teacher Handbook

Author

Jim Walters, M.A., N.B.C.T.

Teacher Created Resources, Inc.
6421 Industry Way
Westminster, CA 92683
www.teachercreated.com

ISBN-1-4206-3949-8

©2005 *Teacher Created Resources, Inc.*

Reprinted, 2005*

Made in U.S.A.

Table of Contents

Being a Professional Substitute Teacher

At Home

- Answer the phone on the first ring. The person calling is very busy and usually has many positions that need to be filled that morning.

- Be cheerful when you get a call at 5:00 A.M. Keep in mind that there is a person at the other end of the phone who had to get up much earlier than you in order to call you.

- Keep a pad of paper and pencil by the bed to write down the assignment. It's very easy to forget something when you have just woken up.

- Arrange your clothes the night before. Make sure you have all the items you would need and that they are clean and freshly pressed.

When You Arrive at School

- Arrive at your assignment earlier than requested, especially if it's the first time you've been in that particular teacher's class. Have your Sub Grab-Bag (see page 12) with you. Check in with the school secretary and see if there are any duties, assemblies, or anything else unexpected that you might need to do.

- Treat the school secretary with the utmost respect. He or she can be your best friend. If you are going to make anyone angry with you at the school, don't let it be the secretary.

- Obtain any keys that might be necessary and check the teacher's mailbox for announcements, attendance sheets, and so on.

- Obtain the bell schedule, in case your teacher has not provided it for you in his or her notes.

- Find the location of the restrooms and the teachers' lounge.

- Look around at the physical set-up of the room. Find the plans, rules, evaluation chart, and supplies you will need.

- Follow the plans that are left for you. Don't disregard them and do your own thing. If you have questions, ask other grade-level teachers.

- Write your name and the assignments on the chalkboard.

- Have an activity ready for students to do as soon as they enter the room.

- Finally, go next door and meet that teacher. Ask if you can send a student to his or her room, if necessary. This isn't showing weakness—it's just the opposite: it says that you are preparing for any challenge.

Being a Professional Substitute Teacher

Moving Through the Day

- If a seating chart is not available, make one as you take attendance. (See page 28 for information on seating charts.)
- Learn the names of as many students as possible. Learn at least a few names immediately.
- Follow the teacher's lesson plans as closely as possible. Supplement with your own activities only after the assigned work is done.
- Let only one student out of class at a time, with a hall pass of some sort. Bring your own, if necessary.
- Take notes throughout the day about incidents you want to share with the classroom teacher. Whenever you're unsure of what action to take, err on the side of caution.
- During the break time, go into the teacher's lounge and meet other teachers. If they seem "standoffish", ask questions about them. People are often willing to talk about themselves if you show interest. Tell them you are available if they should need someone to substitute. This is how you get more job assignments.
- Walk around the room. Students understand that if you move into an area of the room, you will take possession of it. On the other hand, if you never walk around the room, you're letting them know that they are in charge there. Also, moving around the room allows you to speak to the students for both control and social purposes.

Before You Leave

- Before the children leave, have them clean the room. This can be fun and easy. If, for example, you are reading a story or doing quiet seat work the last part of the day, ask for two or three volunteers to clean up the floor. You will be surprised at how well they will do because they were "chosen."
- Complete a teacher report form. Include a list of students who were absent or went home early.
- Make the classroom look as it did when you arrived. Make it even neater, if possible. Teachers love this.
- Grade any work you can. If you are in doubt as to what the teacher wants, leave it, but make sure it is stacked neatly. Try to keep track of who finished what and leave that information for the teacher, too.
- Leave a full report about what you did and did not cover as far as lesson plans are concerned. Also mention student behavior, especially positive things. If any major negative episodes occur, write down what happened and also let another teacher or the aide know about the incident.
- Go through the office and return the key. When you are there, ask if you will be needed the next day. Tell the secretary how much you enjoyed your time at the school or maybe what you learned during the day and how you hope to return for another assignment. Even if you are exhausted, don't let her know: she's had a hard day, too.

Tips for Substitute Teachers

By its very nature, substitute teaching can be hard work. As a substitute teacher, you do not have time to develop a rapport with your students. Often, it's a one-day assignment, and so the students don't feel entirely comfortable with you. They are used to their classroom teacher, and suddenly they get this "stranger" for one day. All that disruption can become more than they want to handle. Here are a few tips to help make your day go more smoothly and to help ensure that you will be asked to teach again at a particular school:

❑ **Always follow the classroom teacher's lesson plans (or whatever substitute instructions he or she has left).** The top complaint heard from teachers about substitutes is that they do not follow the lesson plans. If you can't figure them out or they are inadequate, tell the regular teacher what you've done and why (in a nice way, of course).

❑ **Take time before school to review material that is unfamiliar.** If that still does not help, try to find another teacher who will explain it to you. The second most common complaint teachers have about substitutes is that they do not know anything about the subject and confuse the students. Make every attempt to understand the lessons. If you don't understand something, you can pick out someone who seems unusually bright and ask him or her to explain it to the class.

❑ **Make a discipline plan.** Get input from classroom teachers and principals before the final draft is made. Then when subbing, show it to the principal of the school beforehand and ask if he or she thinks it's appropriate. Then follow through with it in the classroom. (Another common complaint about substitutes is lack of classroom control.) You might need to have two "rule" posters: one for elementary and another for junior high and high school. You should have a maximum of five rules on your poster. Post these rules at the front of classroom before the students arrive.

❑ **Bring some fun extra activities the students can do when—and only when—their work is done.** There are many fun handouts included in this book, so look for something that is appropriate for the grade level you are teaching. Other ideas might be pictures to color, dot-to-dot sheets, word searches, mazes, etc.

❑ **Leave a note for the teacher at the end of the day.** Let the classroom teacher know how the day went. Did the students struggle with a lesson? If so, let the teacher know. Did the students have fun with an activity? Again, tell the teacher. Remember to include the positives of the day, as well as the negatives.

❑ **Make sure the room is in order before leaving.** Something else that can frustrate the classroom teachers is when they can't find books and papers when they return. Make an effort to stack handed-in assignments in a neat and organized manner where the teacher can easily find them. Put all books away where they were at the start of the day. Be sure the room looks orderly. The easiest way to make sure the room is clean is to ask the students to clean up the floor and put things away. Generally, they know where things go. If they don't want to do this, then make it a contest, such as Table 1 vs. Table 2.

What the Regular Classroom Teacher Wants From You

Remember, when classroom teachers are unhappy with the condition a substitute has left their classroom, they can (and will) request that a particular substitute teacher never again work in their classroom. On the other hand, if they are happy with what they find when they return, they will often request you for the next time they have to be absent. Here are a few ways to gain favorable notice with your students' regular teacher:

1. Follow the Lesson Plans

This is a big one with the regular classroom teacher. Follow plans, if at all possible. If the outline of the day doesn't make sense, then ask someone for help. When that approach fails, consult your Sub Grab-Bag (page 12). If you have planned ahead, you can pull out something that is appropriate and go with that.

2. Be Flexible With the Children

Neither you nor the students are used to working with each other. You've both come in with certain expectations that may or may not be realistic. The more flexible you are able to be, the easier your day will go. Take "extras," especially a familiar book to read to the children if time permits. Use your ingenuity.

3. Grading Papers

Of course teachers love for you to correct papers if you understand what they want. Sometimes this is easy, as with math or spelling. Other subjects, such as creative writing, can be difficult because you don't know the teacher's standards. The best advice is to do the finest job you can. If it can be done simply and easily, then go ahead and do it. You will be highly appreciated.

4. Discipline

Often, discipline is the number-one issue for the substitute teacher. If you can't control the students, you can't teach them. As stated before, the teacher may have told you the normal discipline plan for the class. Whenever possible, use it. If that doesn't work, start changing the rules. Whenever you do change, tell the students what you are doing. Let them know you expect them to follow your rules even if they are somewhat different from those of the regular classroom teacher.

What the Principal Wants From You

It is also important, of course, to create a favorable impression with the school's principal. Here are a few tips for achieving that goal:

1. Discipline

Once again, this is a key issue. Whenever possible, all discipline should be in the classroom. Don't send them to the office unless the offense is very serious. Don't be afraid to call out for help when you need it. Principals expect a good substitute teacher to do this. Next, use the discipline plan the students are used to, if possible. If that doesn't work, try your own various methods.

2. Promptness

It is definitely to your advantage to be at the school at least half an hour before the students arrive. Why? Because you will need that time to meet the staff and get prepared. Remember to assume that everything that can go wrong will go wrong—and at the worst possible time. You may not be able to find the lesson plans, or you may have recess duty that morning before school.

3. Following Lesson Plans

Just as this is important to the classroom teacher, it's also one of the first things the principal wants to see. Principals are ultimately responsible for the overall educational process that takes place at the school. They need your help to keep the class on track.

4. Dress Appropriately

Guest teachers are expected to dress better than the regular teaching staff. This may seem unfair, but consider this fact: you need all the help possible to be the authority in an unknown situation. Having a professional appearance can only help you.

5. Personality

Principals want substitute teachers who are pleasant but firm. Be enthusiastic during the day and avoid a babysitting attitude.

Exercising Professional Judgment

Use the information on this page and on page 11 to help you to exercise appropriate judgement in a number of classroom scenarios.

Responding to the Call: Substitute-teacher callers usually start their work very early in the morning, and they respond well to others who are courteous. Many districts are now using computerized systems. Either way, you may get the call very early in the morning or even the night before. Be prepared for this contact. If it is necessary to refuse an assignment, do so as politely as possible.

A Change of Clothing in Your Car: You never know what is waiting for you when you get to your assignment. Field trips, student activities, and other unanticipated educational activities may occur. Always carry tennis shoes and clothing suitable for physical-education activities in your car in preparation for these events.

Ability to Relate to Others: You need to be able to work well with others to be successful in this field. Substitute teachers should treat students, parents, secretaries, classified staff, teachers, administrators, and all others with whom they come into contact in a friendly, courteous, and respectful manner. Those people who are negative, have no sense of humor, or are inflexible seldom get invited back.

Negativity: It's a big mistake to speak negatively about the job. When teachers hear you talking this way, they assume you will do the same thing about their class. This is one good reason for them not to request you in the future.

Look and Act Like a Teacher: You are no longer a student: you are a professional and need to dress accordingly. Shirts, ties, dress pants and dress shoes (unless teaching a physical activity) are most appropriate for men. Appropriately-cut dresses, blouses, pant suits, and women's slacks are appropriate for women. Short dresses, low-cut blouses, blouses which expose the navel, unusual hair colorings and pierced body parts (other than ears), T-shirts, or pants with holes in them are normally not appropriate. Look at the rest of the staff to gauge the dress code.

Assignment Preparation: Know where you are going each day. If necessary, draw yourself a map to each school. In most instances, substitute teachers will find that the classroom teacher left detailed lesson plans. However, there are times when you will need your "bag of tricks," so come prepared. Plan on arriving early and checking into the school office immediately upon arrival.

Following Classroom Lesson Plans: Most regular classroom teachers leave detailed substitute teacher lesson plans and expect you to follow them closely.

Instructional Aides & Use of Students: It's really nice if you have an instructional aide, but this is usually not the case. If one comes in and you didn't expect him or her, ask what is usually done and follow the aide's lead. Students are usually an excellent source of reliable information, so use a few of the more responsible ones.

Emergency Plans & Exits: An emergency plan should be posted somewherein the room. Find it and know what you are expected to do in the event that something should occur.

Exercising Professional Judgment *(cont.)*

Confidentiality: Always maintain confidentiality concerning the school and students. This is not only a legal responsibility: it is essential for the protection of students and families. If you need to talk to someone, seek out an administrator at the school right away. (See pages 16–18 for a detailed list of the legal responsibilities of substitute teachers.)

Grading Student Papers: Teachers love it when they come back to piles of corrected work. If this is possible, then do it. If you don't know the teacher's standards or how to correct something, then, by all means, leave it. At the very least, student papers should be organized, so the classroom teachers can more readily grade them upon their return.

Use of Controversial Materials: Don't show your own movie to the class unless it has a legitimate educational purpose and is closely related to the curriculum. Even so, it must always be rated "G."

Student Use of Computers and the Internet: The Internet contains some material that is inappropriate for student use. Chat rooms should be avoided unless the teacher's directions stipulate otherwise. If this is the case, the students must be very closely monitored. If there is no direction from the regular classroom teacher, ask another teacher. Always use your best judgment in this area.

Leaving a Report at the End of the Day: The regular classroom teachers really want to know how your day went. There are forms in this book (pages 216–217) that will help you to leave the type of information they need to see.

Physical Contact with Students: This is a dangerous issue. Firstly, it is against the law in most states to use any type of physical punishment with public-school students. Secondly, you should always be very careful when touching students. Let the students initiate it—and even then, less is much better than more. This is an area that can place you at legal and professional risk.

Being Alone with Students: It is not recommended that you keep a student in the room alone with you. If you do find yourself in this situation, keep the door open and keep in plain view of those outside.

Language Barriers: If there is a language barrier, find the classroom aide or another student to help you. Sometimes this isn't possible. In that case, know that the child is probably used to this and is making accommodations whenever possible.

Principal Observation of Substitute Teachers: Many substitute teachers want to be observed by the principal. This is a wonderful opportunity to become known if you are looking for a permanent job. Unfortunately, most principals don't have the time to do this unless you are assigned at their school for a long-term assignment. If this is the case, then be sure to invite him/her in to watch you.

Checking Out at the End of the Day: Remember to turn your classroom keys in to the office and find out if your teaching services are needed the following day.

Sub Grab-Bag

What might you need on the job when you don't know anything about it? This happens every day when you are a substitute teacher. Here's a list of things you should consider having with you on every assignment:

- Paper clips
- Marking pens
- Name tags
- Seating chart forms
- Ream of duplicating paper
- Literature selections
- Emergency lesson plans
- Whistle
- Sun hat or sunscreen
- Jogging shoes or flats for P.E. and recess duty
- Assignment calendar
- Time sheet
- Small cooler or lunch box and thermos
- Change of clothing (in case teaching assignment changes after your arrival)
- Copies of instructional materials that you wish to use with the class
- Index card of P.E. activities (see pages 166–177 for ideas)
- Stickers or ink stamp and pad (primary & elementary levels)
- Cassette tape of classical or easy listening music
- Index card of "sponge" activities for students to use after they finish their assignments (see pages 99–105 for ideas)
- Copy of your own discipline plan (laminated and ready to post)
- Special objects or items that you would like to use with the class that may motivate them during the day
- Teaching journal
- Blank forms of a regular classroom teacher report (to be completed and left at the end of the day)

Substitute Teaching FAQs

The following questions are the ones most frequently asked by substitute teachers.

Question: The only way I find work is to constantly go to the worst schools in the district. I was so stressed that I took my name off their list. Now they call me for special-education classes, and I don't know what I'm doing. Why can't I have the nice normal classes where students want to learn? What should I do?

Answer:

- Sign up with other districts.
- Go to the district office and ask the sub clerk why you aren't called for other schools.
- Stop by the secretary at the end of the day and ask if there is any need for your services tomorrow. Maybe you will have first pick of a good class.
- Take some classes on teaching special-education students and classroom management. The district might offer these classes. Ask.
- If you have the time, visit different schools and look at their special-education classes. This will show you how many are run.

Question: Is there a way to find out which special-education classes are violent? I don't want to teach in that atmosphere.

Answer: Without taking the risk and going in there first, you won't know. When you are at a site, ask what their special-education classes are like. Above all, don't stop doing something like this because of a few unfortunate situations.

Question: Is it OK to wander around the school to look at things during my prep period? Should I stop in at the office and offer to help?

Answer: It's a great idea to walk around and get a feel of the school. However, you should check the school policy on this. If you want to volunteer to work for the office staff, tell them ahead of time what time you will be in.

A few words of caution:

- look like you know where you are going
- don't get involved in discipline situations unless asked
- be quiet
- don't interrupt classes in session.

Question: I worked every day for four weeks and loved it. Now I'm hardly called at all. I'm not aware of any problems and I loved the kids, so what's going on?

Answer: Maybe there were several inservices those first four weeks. Are you struggling with the calendar? Teachers don't usually take days off right before or after holidays. Open up the field where you work. Apply to different districts. A final word: try to refrain from referring to the students as "kids."

Substitute Teaching FAQs (cont.)

Question: What about seating charts? How do I know the students are sitting in the correct seats? Many times I don't have one, and that makes it difficult to take role. It's especially difficult to call on students. What should I do?

Answer: If the teacher has left you a list of students who are especially helpful, ask one of them to make you a seating chart. It will probably be correct. If you want to make sure they are sitting in the correct place, go desk by desk and call their names while watching their faces.

Question: I'm very uncomfortable in the staff lunchroom. Nobody talks to me, and if I enter into a conversation, they look at me as if I don't belong.

Answer: This is an ongoing problem. If they won't start talking to you, then initiate it yourself. Ask questions about them. Show you are interested in what they are doing. People think you are a wonderful conversationalist when you talk about them. As people become more familiar with you, they will make you feel more comfortable.

Question: How do I know if the noise level in the class is correct? I'm afraid that someone will hear us and think I'm not a good teacher because the students are too noisy.

Answer: Get the class working immediately on a quiet learning activity. Tell them before they come into the room what you expect from them. Walk around the room whenever possible to keep them on track. Have a contest for the quietest table of the day. Know your discipline plan and use it. Remember that noise isn't always bad, and you can always close the door.

Question: Help! I've subbed for this class before, but today they are completely out of control. They came in especially wired, and I'm having a really hard time getting them to listen to me.

Answer: Transition time from outdoors is always tricky. Before they come into the room, let them know what you expect. Have something for them to do immediately. If you are still having problems, stop and read them a story. They need several minutes to break the pattern.

Question: What if I can't find things the teacher left for me? Should I ask the teacher next door to help, or will that make me look incompetent?

Answer: Get to the school at least half an hour before class starts. The more time you have to find and figure out things, the better you will be. If something is definitely not there, by all means, ask.

Question: Am I expected to grade papers? I don't know what the teacher's expectations are, and I don't feel confident enough in my own experience.

Answer: Do what you can. The teacher really appreciates anything you can do. Don't feel you need to stay late or make value judgments about students' work when you aren't qualified.

Substitute Teaching FAQs *(cont.)*

Question: I just saw the teacher I subbed for, and she hardly talked to me at all. Should I be worried?

Answer: If everything went well while you were there, don't be concerned.

Question: I don't ever want to go back to some schools. How can I say that without hurting my chances of getting work?

Answer: First of all, it's normal that you have a list of schools where you won't teach. It happens all the time. Having said that, you must realize that those are the ones who typically need subs and that you are cutting yourself off from a lot of potential work. Just tell the sub clerk/automated system that you will not be available at a particular school.

Question: What are the things a teacher wishes to hear from their "Substitute Teacher Report" at the end of the day?

Answer: The teacher wants to know the following information:

- work which was not completed and why (e.g., not enough time, impromptu assembly program, etc.)
- students who were problematic and how
- any concerns about the type of work left for the students
- overall class behavior and attitude toward the sub
- a folder of work collected from the students
- names of students who were absent.

Question: When I write my name on the board, do I ask the kids to call me by my first name or by Miss/Mrs./Mr. and my last name?

Answer: It is recommended that you ask your students to address you as Mr., Miss, Mrs., or Ms. (whichever you prefer) and your last name. You need a professional distance from your students.

Question: What's the best way to remember the names of the children that I will be teaching?

Answer: Take time to memorize their names, if you want. If you have a seating chart, look at it constantly and memorize names to faces. Some substitutes use name tags and even carry laminated name cards and have the children write their names on them with dry-erase pens.

Question: What do I do when I'm having trouble getting into the copy room to make assignments for the day?

Answer: Trying to make copies right before school starts can be a nightmare. The best advice is to get to school early and do it immediately. If you have been to the school many times and know the secretary, you might be able to get her to run some things off for you.

Legal Responsibilities

Use the following list as a basic guide. Legal responsibilities may vary for specific states or school districts. This list has been included to make substitute teachers aware of potential dangers and responsibilities, and it should not be construed as legal advice.

Theory of Common Law—Court rulings state that schools have a special relationship with students and have a legal duty to protect them from foreseeable harm. They've ruled that schools be held liable for injuries to students if all three of the following elements are present:

- a duty of reasonable care is lacking
- a breach of duty that is the proximate cause of the damage
- actual damage to the plaintiff.

Loco Parentis—This states that schools are expected to act in the place of parents while the student is in school.

Due Process—Courts have held that education is a property right. Student property rights may not be abridged without observing students' legal due-process rights. The guarantee of a fair and impartial hearing must be afforded all students.

Respondeat Superior (**"Let the Master Pay"**)—The school districts are held responsible for the actions of their employees when that person is carrying out the duties of his or her job. If an employee isn't acting within the scope of his or her job, then that individual is solely responsible for their actions, not the school district.

Theory of Reasonableness—Courts will look to see if school personnel acted in a reasonable and careful manner under the circumstances if a student is injured.

Degree of Foreseeable Harm—Courts will try to learn if the injury to a student could have been anticipated and prevented. To what extent could the school have known that something might happen under those circumstances?

Food Allergies—Be very careful when using candy or other edible treats as rewards. Food allergies—especially to peanuts, which can be found in trace amounts in many foods that do not appear to contain peanuts—can be very dangerous. It is best to avoid giving food to students.

> *If you walk into a classroom and find that the exits are blocked by desks, it is your responsibility to move them and create a safe environment for children.*

Injuries to Students—If the child is injured and you aren't sure whether or not to move him, then don't. Call the school office immediately for help and let them make the decision. Attend to the injured student, and send another student for help.

Legal Responsibilities *(cont.)*

Playground Supervision—If a student is seriously injured on the playground, the courts will want to determine if there was proper supervision on the playground and whether or not those individuals were diligent in carrying out their responsibilities. It is necessary to carry out proper safety rules. They will also look to see if the danger was preventable or foreseeable; and if human error did occur, the courts will seek to determine how much, if at all, that error led to or contributed to the incident.

Student Supervision Requirements—In most states, except during lunch periods, teachers or other certified staff must be able to see every student and assume responsibility for their supervision. Usually classified staff may not legally assume this role except during lunch periods.

> *Never leave your students unsupervised. If you need to step out, find another adult to watch the class.*

Leaving Students Unattended—Teachers should not leave students in classrooms unattended without certified supervision. Teachers are responsible for all students under their charge and are legally responsible for the welfare of missing students. Missing students should be reported to the school office immediately.

Release of Students—Release students to adults only with proper authorization from the school office. This is especially true if you are not sure they are the legal guardians of the student. Send the individual to the school office for written authorization before the student is released.

Letting Students Out Early—Check with school administrators before you let students out early. Letting them out early can often result in students being unsupervised. If that happens, the school and teacher(s) are legally responsible. If you first have permission from the administration, then you must also supervise the students you let out early.

Student Detention During Recess or the Noon Break—Check the school policy before you withhold a student's recess or nutrition break and before you require him/her to stay after school.

School Visitors—Most schools require visitors to report to the school office prior to visiting classrooms or the playground. If you observe individuals at the school who you believe are unauthorized, report them to the school office immediately. Most schools will provide visitors with name tags or written authorization.

Confidentiality—Do not give out any information about a student to a person outside the school system. Instead, refer this person to the school principal. It's important that you be diligent in protecting the privacy rights of students and families.

Legal Responsibilities (cont.)

Sexual Harassment—Sexual harassment (use of sexually explicit language, requests for sexual favors, sexually graphic materials/language, or the creation of a sexually hostile work or learning environment) between students, between staff and students, or between staff members is against the law and should be reported immediately to the appropriate school administrator.

Use of Physical Force—Physical force should only be used in an emergency in which it prevents some type of injury, either to the student or another person. If used, physical force must be limited to the amount of force absolutely necessary to prevent injury. It's also important to avoid placing yourself in danger of injury when supervising students. If you feel your emotions are running high, clasp your hands behind your back as you talk to the student.

Corporal Punishment—Most school districts prohibit the use of physical punishment. Plan on never using it.

Child Abuse Reporting—If a teacher even suspects child abuse, then it must be reported to the proper legal authorities. They will help you through further notification process.

> *If as a substitute teacher you suspect the child has been abused, you should report it to the school nurse, counselor, or site lead administrator.*

Student Searches—Earlier it was said that teachers serve *in loco parentis* for students, but this doesn't mean they may search those students without reasonable suspicion. Teachers are not to conduct body searches on students of the opposite gender at any time. Even same-sex student body searches should only be done when reasonable suspicion exists and when at least one staff member is present to serve as a witness. Never conduct a strip search: they are strictly illegal.

Weapons and Drugs—Most school districts have a zero-tolerance policy regarding weapons and drugs in schools. Any student suspected of being in possession of weapons or drugs or under the influence of drugs is in violation of the law, and you must notify the school administration immediately.

Students on Medication—Students may not take any medication without being under the immediate supervision of appropriately designated and trained staff. Students who bring medications to class have to take them to the school nurse immediately.

Personal Use of School Property—School property belongs to the public and may not be used for personal use.

Chapter 2
Classroom Management

Introduction

When you hear the words "classroom management," you might connect it with classroom discipline. Although they are used interchangeably much of the time, they are actually two different topics. Discipline involves trying to change the student's behavior; classroom management is simply how things are done.

As Dr. Marvin Marshall of Teachers.Net Gazette explains, "Discipline is about impulse management and self-control. Classroom management has to do with procedures, structure, and routines. Discipline is the student's responsibility. Classroom management—the key to efficient instruction—is the teacher's responsibility." The reason these two terms are often treated as synonyms is that you have to set up how you want the classroom to function in order to get the students to behave.

This section will address five questions (detailed below and on pages 20–21). If you can plan for each of them, you should have a successful classroom-management program.

1. What can I do to build an environment where students want to participate and cooperate with the teacher and each other to achieve the goals of the class?

Children want to be part of an environment—learning or otherwise—that is engaging, entertaining, and informative. It's really hard to do that all the time, but that's what they are striving for. Of the three, "entertaining" is the least essential, but it will make the difference between a lesson that sparkles and one that is truly boring.

First, make sure everyone knows what is expected from him or her. The first thing students need to do is treat you as a professional. When you are ready to teach, they need to be ready to listen. This will probably not come naturally to them. After you have been teaching for a long time, you will see how much time can be wasted this way. Typically, students don't mind talking louder than you because they feel that whatever they have to say is very important. Demand attention before you even begin. Develop a signal that will get their attention right away. Don't worry about wasting a few seconds or even a minute waiting for the class to calm down. It is well worth the effort and will save you a lot of time in the long run.

Monitor your own voice. Keep it at a level that can be heard when they are quiet but not much more than that. The quietest class in the school will probably be with the teacher who has laryngitis. As a matter of fact, talk less. Simply looking at a student, saying his or her name, and then moving closer to him or her (only as many steps as necessary) is much more effective than stating whatever you want them to do or not to do. When they see you moving toward them, they usually do exactly what you wanted them to do all along.

	Possible Signals	
• two claps	• ring a bell	• count down
• thumbs up	• shaker	• hand signal
• lights off	• toy whistle	

Introduction (cont.)

2. What rules will help students understand the way I want the class to run?

Keep your rules simple and positive. Make a list of general policies first. What are the things you absolutely must have? An example of this might be: "Students will feel comfortable and safe in my classroom" and "Students will do their best effort." From this you make your rules. Keep them positive. So, instead of saying, "No drinks while I am teaching," say "Drinks only when I'm not addressing the class." Instead of "no gum chewing," use "Leave gum at home." Use only three to five rules so that the children can remember them.

One of the biggest mistakes new teachers make is when they don't ask the students to practice what they expect. Take time to rehearse what you want. If you want their attention when you ring a bell, don't start teaching before they can give you their attention.

Using a signal to get the student's attention is something that the substitute teacher needs to teach early on. You need to develop a non-verbal clue that will alert the group that you want their attention. These can be facial expressions, body posture, or hand signals. Care should be given in choosing the type of cue you use in your classroom, and be sure to take the time to explain what you want to students to do when you use your cue. Here is an example of applying a rule:

Walking in line

- ❖ Challenge students to walk in a perfectly straight line.
- ❖ Tell them it is a contest between boys and girls.
- ❖ Ask students to walk with their hands behind their back.
- ❖ After you've gotten a chance to know the class, put one of the more responsible students in charge of keeping a straight line.

---

3. How will I enforce rules and still maintain a positive relationship with my students?

New teachers are often known as being extreme in their discipline. They are either very, very strict or far too lenient. You are going to have to find a way to be strict without painting yourself into a corner. Your first support should be your own preparation. Always come to the assignment equipped for anything. There are lessons, fillers, games, and plenty of ideas contained in this book. It is important to be ready in case there isn't a teaching lesson provided for you.

Next, teach the rules and procedures you want. Don't just announce them before you enforce them; make sure everyone is aware of what is expected.

If you have a potentially explosive student, put your hands behind your back and remain calm and in control. Listen, use the student's name, and respond empathetically, "Nevertheless, I want you to…." With the appropriate use of respect, eye contact, and facial expression, this will usually defuse the situation. You are trying to take care that the student is not rewarded for misbehavior by becoming the focus of attention.

Introduction *(cont.)*

4. What incentives can I use to increase the motivation of my students?

It's best to tell the students exactly what you want—and even to describe the action they are to take. Don't assume they will be able to picture it. Give them a picture.

Classroom discipline is easy: just give the students what they want. Of course, you are going to limit the options from which they may choose. Many like to give out prizes, but buying things can be very expensive on a substitute teacher's salary, so look for things that don't cost anything. The number-one rule with rewards is that if the children view them as important, they will work.

Author Harry Wong suggests that the teacher draw a big heart on the board. Inside that heart is placed the names of all the students in the class on separate pieces of paper. If a student violates a rule, kindly remove his or her paper and place it outside the heart. Encourage the student to return to the heart. This can be done with any shape, as you may find that the higher grades won't respond well to the heart shape. Change it any way you need to.

Simple rewards are the best because they are understood, valued, and easy to administer. They can be a smile, a high five, a pat, a handshake, or a simple word of encouragement. One of the most effective rewards in many cases is a call to their parents. If the classroom has a phone, ask the child to call their parent and tell them that the teacher is really pleased with his or her behavior (or performance, grade, etc.) and wants them to know. It costs nothing, is easy to administer, and will work wonders for you.

5. What support systems can I build to help me manage my class?

Always start your day with something for the students to do. Whether it's on their desk or on the board, they should know exactly what to do the minute they enter the room. If you need board work, consider writing four math problems or perhaps three sentences for the students to complete or correct.

Next, you need to move around the room. Author Fred Jones says that the room is divided into three distinct areas: the nearby green zone, where the students are actively listening and involved; the yellow zone, which is usually 10–15 feet from you and where they may be involved when they think you are watching; and the back part of the class, the red zone, where they are pretty much playing around or daydreaming. When you move around, you change the boundaries of these groups, and students who were in the yellow or red zones must start to pay attention. You own the part of the room that you possess.

Techniques that Backfire

Avoid the following techniques when dealing with students:

- Raising your voice
- Insisting on having the last word
- Using tense body language, such as rigid posture or clenched hands
- Using degrading, insulting, humiliating, or embarrassing put-downs
- Using sarcasm
- Attacking the student's character
- Using physical force
- Drawing unrelated persons into the conflict
- Having a double standard—making students do what you say, not what you do
- Making assumptions
- Backing the student into a corner
- Pleading or bribing
- Generalizing about students by making remarks such as, "All of you kids are the same."
- Making unsubstantiated accusations
- Holding a grudge
- Mimicking the student
- Making comparisons with siblings or other students
- Commanding, demanding, dominating
- Buying off students who are disruptive

Guidelines

- Deal only with what you can see.
- Be specific when negotiating rules.
- Privileges and consequences should be meaningful to the students.
- Never argue. Concentrate on the behavior and consequences.

Important Points to Remember

> ☞ **Remember:** It is important for you, as a substitute teacher, to establish what you expect and what the students can expect from you at the beginning of the day. You need to be perceived by students as confident, in charge, and fair.

Respecting Students

Remember that each student is someone who wants to be treated as a unique individual, regardless of how smart they are, what language they speak, what country they are from, or how well they dress. Students respect adults who respect them.

Staying In Control

Even in times of extreme stress, it is very important that the substitute teacher be in control of his or her emotions. Show the students how they are to act even when you are about to blow your stack. When you lose your temper, it makes it that much harder to get control of a difficult situation. At this point, the students are only watching to see what is going to happen to you.

Eye Contact

Don't be afraid to look students directly in the eye in most circumstances. The exception would be if you are in a volatile one-on-one situation, where it might be considered too intimidating.

Raising Your Voice

Raise your voice only when you are using it as an instructional tool. If you are trying to get control, you should have an attention signal you've taught the students. Generally speaking, the quieter you stay, the quieter the class will be. Try using a stage whisper to get their attention when they start talking. People naturally respond to whispering because it sounds like they will learn a secret.

Use of a Whistle

Use a whistle when you are working with students outside only. This is very effective during physical education but should never be used in the classroom.

Establishing Standards of Conduct

As soon as you meet your students in the morning, you need to start teaching what you expect from them. If you first greet them on the playground, then give your expectations right there. Set firm, fair, and consistent standards for work and behavior. Students respect someone who is coming from a position of strength and appears to be reasonable.

Important Points to Remember (cont.)

Logical Consequences for Student Behavior

Students need to know that there are logical consequences for their actions. If they do a good job, they can expect to be rewarded with a positive reaction. Conversely, if they break one of the rules, they are choosing to accept the natural consequences that go along with that. The closer you can get the punishment to fit the crime, the more the student will understand why he or she is receiving it. For example, if the student is caught throwing spit wads across the room, then he or she can choose to clean up the floor during recess.

Positive Reinforcement

Everyone loves positive reinforcement. It instinctively tells us that we are good people. Students do not respond well to sarcasm, even when used as humor, unless you have a relationship with them that allows that. Praising desired behavior is much more effective than punishing undesired behavior. It creates a positive room environment and makes the day that much nicer for you.

Praise and Correction Guides

Generally, it is much more effective to correct students privately than publicly. Unless the situation needs immediate attention due to safety factors, you should speak to the student one-on-one. When you embarrass students in front of their peers, you are simply creating a situation where they often respond by acting out even more. Remember, the student has a relationship with the class already—whereas you do not. At the elementary level, it is generally acceptable to praise a particular student in front of other students; but at the middle school and high school levels, individual praise normally needs to be done privately, while group praise is done publicly. Make sure any praise you give is real and not contrived. Normally you should use as few words as possible when giving praise to an individual or the class, and it should take only a few seconds each time.

Surprising Students

Surprising your students may work when you are getting their attention during instruction. However, if you are giving directions, they need to be clear and understandable. Since these students don't know you, they need to feel safe in your presence. Surprising them with some form of discipline will usually prove to be both ineffective and disruptive. You don't want to create new problems for yourself.

Unstructured Student Time

Unstructured time is generally not productive time. The more the students feel free to choose an activity, the greater chance they have of making bad choices. Have work on their desks or on the board when they walk in, and have something else available for them to do when they are finished with their assignments.

Important Points to Remember (cont.)

Correlation of Success and Student Behavior

If discipline problems are increasing, look to see if the work is simply too advanced for these students. Classes tend to get off track if they are frustrated. At the same time, if you give assignments that are too easy, students may become bored and also begin to act out. As the teacher, you need to constantly check to see how they are doing by walking around and offering help. Assisting students who are having trouble and adjusting the level of difficulty of the work will go a long way to ensure proper classroom management. Increasing the difficulty of the work or providing alternative learning assignments to students who have demonstrated mastery of the assignment will help to prevent boredom and classroom disruptions.

Proximity & Classroom Management

There is a direct correlation between how far the teacher is from the student and proper behavior. The further away from them that you are, the less likely they are to be paying attention. The trick is to keep moving. That way the zones constantly change and you have more control.

Supervising Students from the Back of the Classroom

Don't be afraid to supervise your students from the back of the room. This is especially effective during a film, when the room is dark.

Typical Classroom Rules

Typical elementary- and middle-school classroom rules include the following:

- Keep your feet, hands, and objects to yourself.
- Raise your hand and wait for permission before you speak out.
- Remain in your seat unless you have permission to get up.
- No put-downs or name calling.
- No student will stop another student from learning.

Severe violations, resulting in instant referrals to the principal's office, would include the following:

- fighting
- possession of drugs
- possession of weapons
- physical threats
- constant disruption
- defiance

Typically, high-school-student rules will vary from elementary- and middle-school rules only slightly. When you speak to high school students about your rules, do so in a way that reflects the increased level of their maturity.

Important Points to Remember (cont.)

Ignore

Sometimes you will need to ignore minor infractions. Ignore and the behavior usually passes. Whenever possible, you want to control these small problems without anyone else even noticing. If the undesired behavior persists, you will need to use more direct and forceful intervention strategies.

Parent/Guardian Teacher Contact

It's important to students that their parents approve of their behavior at school. A nice tool for contacting parents is the telephone found in many classes. If you feel students deserve an extra pat on the back, allow them to call home and talk to their parent. On the other hand, if the child is causing a problem, he or she may also need to call home. If you do this, keep it as positive as possible. Try the message, "Mrs. Smith, Johnny is having some trouble settling down today and needs some encouragement. I appreciate your support."

Number of Students Out of Their Seats

Unless you are doing an educational activity that requires it, it isn't recommended that more than one or two students be out of their seats at any given time. Make it a general policy that no one gets out of their seat if you are instructing the class.

Student Use of the Restroom and Drinking Fountains

Expect students to get their drinks and to use the restroom during their breaks. If someone needs to use the restroom, give him or her a time limit (2–5 minutes) and look at your watch. This way you know they won't take advantage of the time situation.

Isolating Students

It's perfectly alright to isolate a student when he or she becomes disruptive. Make sure this student stays in your line of sight. Never put students outside the room where you can't see them. If you do, you are putting yourself in a very vulnerable situation.

Arguing with Students

Students will sometimes want to argue with you when you make a decision. It's okay to discuss something privately, but if you feel the student only wants to argue, say, "I don't argue with students." Then send him/her away.

Important Points to Remember *(cont.)*

Dignifying Students

Students will generally accept fair and reasonable rules and consequences when they know that the teacher is genuinely concerned about their well-being. Students should not be singled out or used as examples. When you have a very difficult day with a student, it is important that before the student leaves for the day you have an opportunity to tell the child that you care for him or her. They will be much less willing to cause you further trouble.

Desired Teacher Characteristics

Always conduct yourself as a professional, an authority figure, and a role model for the students. Teachers should be characterized as caring, capable, and responsive to the students' needs.

Listen Before You Discipline

If students are going to get into trouble during the day, it generally happens during the break time, when things are much less structured. They will want to tell you their problem; and very often it becomes a drawn-out affair, with the students trying to give you the facts. Whenever possible, listen to the witnesses and make an educated decision about what happened. Generally, the incident occurred because some child acted immaturely. Tell them what you think the facts are and then discipline accordingly. They will let you know if you got it all wrong.

Seating Charts

The regular classroom teacher should have left you a seating chart. It's very important that you know students' names so you can address them personally. If you don't have a seating chart, make one as soon as the students start their seatwork. See page 28 for more about seating charts.

Logical Consequences for Rules Infractions

It is difficult to identify in advance appropriate disciplinary consequences for every circumstance that might arise in a school environment. Whenever possible, use the discipline policy and consequences set up by the regular classroom teacher. Typical consequences might include the following:

- name on the board
- loss of recess time
- sending the child next door
- a call to the parents/guardian.

Only send the student to the office if there is a major infraction of the rules such as fighting, talking back to the teacher, possession of drugs or a weapon, or dangerous behavior in the classroom.

Seating Chart

When the students enter the room, have something for them to do on their desks. Make sure they know exactly what you expect from them before they come in. If they don't do this as well as you would like, there's nothing wrong with asking them to quietly stand and file out to try again.

As soon as possible, take roll and make a seating chart if there isn't one for you. The seating chart is one of the best classroom management tools you can have. When a seating chart is established, you will have begun the process of holding the students accountable for their actions. This tells the class that the teacher is in charge of the physical environment of the room, as well as the academic environment. This understanding is particularly useful when dealing with "kinesthetic" students, those who often first need discipline.

One of the easiest ways to make a seating chart is to use sticky notes. Place one of these on each student's desk and immediately ask the students to write their names on them. Collect them and arrange them in a file folder in the same configuration as the desks in the room.

With these charts, you can check daily attendance, record homework, monitor participation, and document student behavior. Once you are able to hold students accountable for their personal behavior, you will have the upper hand on classroom discipline.

Sample Seating Chart

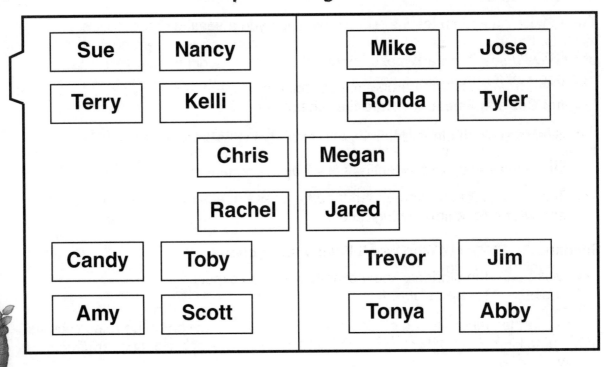

Challenging Scenarios

It's inevitable that you are going to have challenging scenarios in your substituting career. It is the nature of children to test the limits. In the broad scheme of things, this is a good thing because it ultimately helps them develop in a complex society. Of course, that doesn't help you maintain discipline in your classroom. The purpose of this section is to help you think ahead so you can react with confidence in an unexpected situation.

Scenario 1: Students Who Interrupt Learning (i.e., Minor Misbehavior)

➥ Explain what behavior you will recognize, and then stick to it. Totally ignore students who want your attention but don't want to attain it correctly.

➥ Try competition between groups in the room.

➥ Post your consequences for not following the rules.

➥ Move to where the student is sitting.

➥ Carry around a clipboard and look like you are writing down the student's name when he or she is acting out.

Scenario 2: Students Who Never Finish Their Work Even When They Show They Understand It

➥ Try giving them a time limit to do a short portion of the assignment.

➥ Give students a reward if they finish on time (see Rewards on page 39).

➥ Sometimes children want control, so try asking them what they think they can do.

➥ Challenge the students by making it a contest.

➥ If this is a reoccurring problem, post another student to watch him or her for five minutes at a time and reward the other student if the child finishes on time.

➥ Seek help from other teachers who may know this student.

➥ Give time warnings ("Ten minutes left.").

➥ Tell the student that you understand he or she needs more time and that he or she will get that time during recess.

Scenario 3: Students Who Won't Follow Instructions

➥ Make sure the students know exactly what you expect.

➥ Check to see that they understand the assignment before they get to work.

➥ Walk around and check their work. If you see any problems, work privately with them.

➥ If you have a group of students who aren't following instructions, have them work together with you.

Challenging Scenarios *(cont.)*

Scenario 4: The Class that Refuses to Be Quiet, Pay Attention, or Be Cooperative

- Explain exactly what your standards are.

- Move around the room. You own the portion of the room that you possess.

- Call attention to the students who are working effectively.

- When dealing with a problem, do it quietly and privately.

Scenario 5: Transitioning Between Activities

- Tell students what you expect them to do and how long you want it to take.

- Time the transitions.

- Make it a game where students compete with one another for a prize (see Rewards on page 39).

- Rehearse transitions.

- Prepare yourself for transitions as much as possible by having everything ready.

- Pass out supplies and have directions written on the board whenever possible.

- Try shortening the assignment periods so the students don't get bored. If you need to, come back to finish the assignment later.

- Teach the students your attention-getting technique and use it.

- Don't be afraid to send one or two trouble makers to the teacher next door.

Scenario 6: Trouble Getting Their Attention

- Speak in a low tone so that if you do raise your voice, the contrast will be noticed immediately.

- Create a signal that will alert students that you want their attention. Signals can include the following: clap three times, turn on and off the lights, ring a bell, give the thumbs-up sign and have students mimic you, count from five to one, etc.

Challenging Scenarios *(cont.)*

Scenario 7: Students Switching Seats

- Have work for students to do as soon as they come into the room and ask them to put their names on it.

- As they are doing this, go around and make your own seating chart using the names they put on their papers.

- Tell them that you are going to leave a note telling the teacher the students with good behavior and those with bad behavior based on your seating chart.

- Give them 30 seconds to change seats with no penalties.

Scenario 8: Student Use of Profanity and "Put-Downs"

- Explain your rules to the class immediately.

- If necessary, practice these three phrases:

    "I don't like it when you . . ."

    "It makes me feel . . ."

    "Next time, I want you to . . ."

- Speak privately to the student and explain the consequences of doing this again.

Scenario 9: Fights, Threats, Weapons, and Drugs

- If you come upon a fight, send for help—either another teacher or an administrator.

- If you can determine who is the "underdog," tell him or her to go to the office.

- If weapons of any kind are found, refer the child to the administrator

General Principles of Crisis Intervention

3 Steps to Relieve Stress

1. Take a deep breath.
2. Smile.
3. Give someone a compliment.

Self-Control

If you want to help someone else get control of him- or herself, you must first demonstrate it yourself. It's your calm demeanor that helps the other person to slow down.

Identification

You really need to catch potentially explosive situations as soon as possible. Look for clues such as tone of voice and body language. If you can stop it early, you have a much better chance of limiting any further escalation of the student's behavior.

Communication

The "rule of five" states that during crisis intervention, sentences should be limited to no more than five words, and each word used should be limited to five letters or less. Keep your voice flat and non-threatening. Use the person's name and talk only about the one behavior. Provide a clear directive/realistic choice. Simply tell the student what you want him or her to do, not what he or she is doing wrong. This isn't the time for a power struggle.

Body Language

The most powerful methods of communication are required to penetrate the barriers of panic, rage, or irrational demands. Since speech by itself is among the weakest communication methods, it is important to minimize the use of speech and maximize or exaggerate the use of nonverbal communication.

- Project an image of self-confidence, relaxation (e.g., arms at side), security, and caring.
- Movements should be slow and deliberate.
- Try to maintain a distance of about three feet from the student.
- Establish eye contact and block student's vision/access to the source of confrontation.

Perspective

Keep in mind the phrase "This, too, shall pass." It helps to put things in perspective. Most of the time these intervention techniques will work, but remember you can't be in control of all situations. Keep in mind that you are dealing with someone who is temporarily out of control, and he or she may just need time to see things more clearly.

Provide a Positive
Learning Environment

Instead of . . .	Try
✗ Marking "–4" to indicate four mistakes on a test.	✓ Marking "+6" to show how many answers are correct.
✗ Praising an individual student out loud.	✓ Praising the pupil privately and praising the class publicly.
✗ Putting names of deviants on the board.	✓ Putting names of achievers, good citizens, etc., on the board or on a special chart.
✗ Repeatedly explaining the directions.	✓ Modeling the response desired with a few practice examples.
✗ Nagging the child who is not working.	✓ Praising his or her neighbor who is working well.
✗ Criticizing the class for poor test performance.	✓ Praising the class for what they did correctly. After re-instruction, asking them to see if they can improve their scores the second time around.
✗ Talking at length with a child after his or her misbehavior.	✓ Simply telling the student you were disappointed in his or her behavior. Period. Say, "Remember the rule."
✗ Attending to the same child constantly all day.	✓ Give a specific child lots of attention when he or she is doing the right thing.

Helpful Hints for Maintaining Your Classroom Discipline

❑ Set your rules in very specific behavioral terms. Decide on your priorities—things you would term as "must" behaviors.

❑ Post the rules and go over them in class so that everyone knows exactly what is expected.

❑ When giving individual directions, look at the student, call him or her by name, be close, touch in an appropriate manner (e.g., place the student in a seat), and use appropriate verbal and non-verbal cues.

❑ Use specific, goal-directed messages, such as the following:

➡ "Sit down in your chair now; sit quietly, finish these 10 problems, and do not get up until the bell rings."

➡ "John, stop hitting Sue now, and do not hit anyone else ever again in this class."

❑ Watch out for your susceptibility to students' manipulations, particularly those that you engaged in as a child.

✤ arguing

✤ crying

✤ pouting

Note: When incidents do arise, use the "Incident Documentation" sheet on page 38 to record them.

How to Help Children Feel Good About Themselves

Children view themselves by the way they think other people who are important in their lives feel about them. We, as parents and teachers, must remind ourselves to make sure we are doing all we can to help children feel good about themselves. The following suggestions may be helpful:

- Treat children with respect and expect the same behavior from them.

- Help children find their strengths—they know their weaknesses.

- Encourage children in areas of both strengths and weaknesses.

- Find ways to recognize each child as special. Avoid comparing one child to another.

- Listen to the students to better understand their points of view.

- Invite them to express all their feelings appropriately.

- Make sure that when they make mistakes, they know it is because they did something wrong, not because they are bad persons.

- Help children to discover acceptable ways to behave in areas where they are having difficulty.

- Show that you have confidence in them by giving them jobs to do.

Note: When a problem arises, have the student responsible for the problem fill out one or both of "The Problem Solver" worksheets on pages 36 and 37.

The Problem Solver

Your Name:

Today's Date:

Tell about the problem:

How would you solve it?

The Problem Solver (cont.)

Draw a picture of the problem.

How can you fix the problem?

What will it look like if the problem is solved?

Incident Documentation

Date	Time	Place	Person(s) Involved	Description of Incident	Witness(es)	Intervention Taken

Rewards

Consider giving the following rewards to students who meet expectations. See pages 40–43 for reward forms and tickets that can be handed out to students. Have students fill out one bubble on the incentive charts on pages 44–47 for each positive accomplishment.

Recognition	Privileges	Tangible Rewards
Student-of-the-week award	Library pass	Stars
Recognition in daily announcements	Silent reading time	Stickers
	Help other students	Stamps
Smile	Help teacher	
Pat on the back	Choose day's story	Snacks in the room
Hug	Helper for the day	Grab bag
Display work	Pass out papers	Points for a prize
Standing ovation	Water plants	Popcorn party
	Extra art	Eraser
Round of applause	Extra P.E.	Pencil
Encouraging words	Extra music	Bookmarks
	Choose where to sit	
	Choice of music	Tokens
	Play with special game or toy	Audiovisual treat
	Use new markers	Bonus points
	Go outside for class session (whole class)	Extra-credit grade

Reward Forms

_____
Name

Has Had Terrific
BEE-havior Today!

_____
Date

_____
Teacher

_____
Name

Is Today's Star Student

Congratulations!

_____
Date

_____
Teacher

"Congratulations!" Reward Forms

★ ★ ★ CONGRATULATIONS! ★ ★ ★

_____ Won Our Contest Today!
Name

_____   _____
Date   Teacher

★ ★ ★ CONGRATULATIONS! ★ ★ ★

_____ Won Our Contest Today!
Name

_____   _____
Date   Teacher

★ ★ ★ CONGRATULATIONS! ★ ★ ★

_____ Won Our Contest Today!
Name

_____   _____
Date   Teacher

"Great Job!" Reward Forms

Great Job!

did a great job in class today.

_____
Name

_____   _____
Date   Teacher

Great Job!

did a great job in class today.

_____
Name

_____   _____
Date   Teacher

Great Job!

did a great job in class today.

_____
Name

_____   _____
Date   Teacher

Reward Tickets

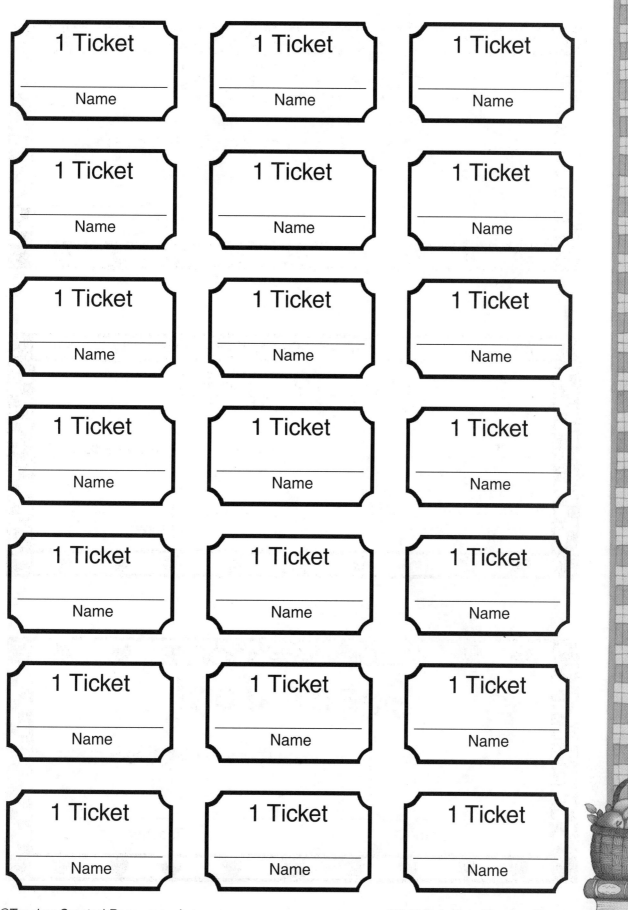

1 Ticket	1 Ticket	1 Ticket
Name	Name	Name
1 Ticket	1 Ticket	1 Ticket
Name	Name	Name
1 Ticket	1 Ticket	1 Ticket
Name	Name	Name
1 Ticket	1 Ticket	1 Ticket
Name	Name	Name
1 Ticket	1 Ticket	1 Ticket
Name	Name	Name
1 Ticket	1 Ticket	1 Ticket
Name	Name	Name
1 Ticket	1 Ticket	1 Ticket
Name	Name	Name

Painter's Palette Incentive Charts

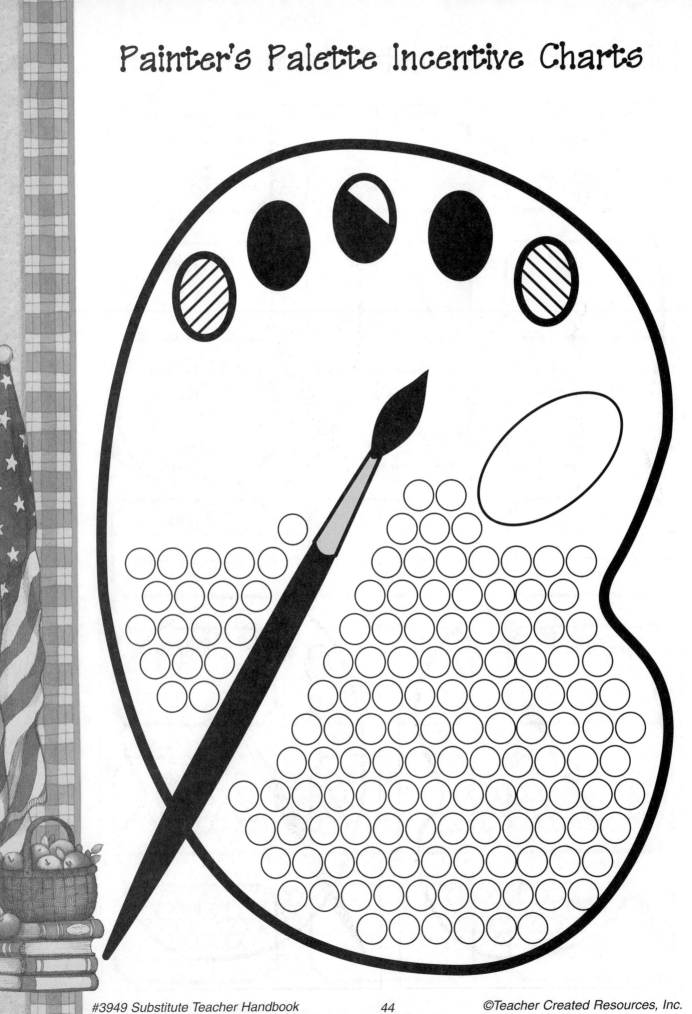

Mini Painter's Palette Incentive Charts

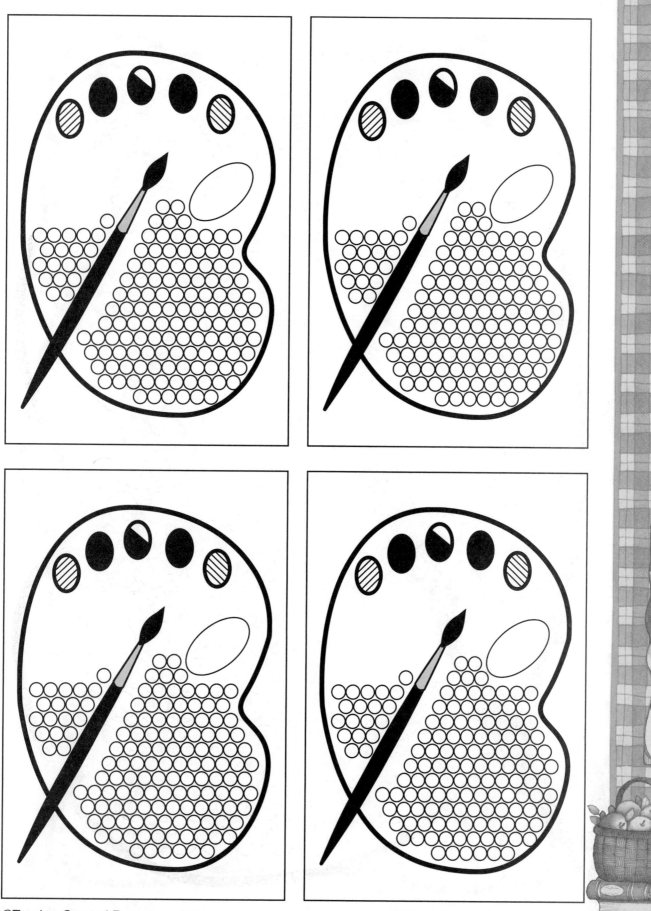

Animal Incentive Charts

MIni Animal Incentive Charts

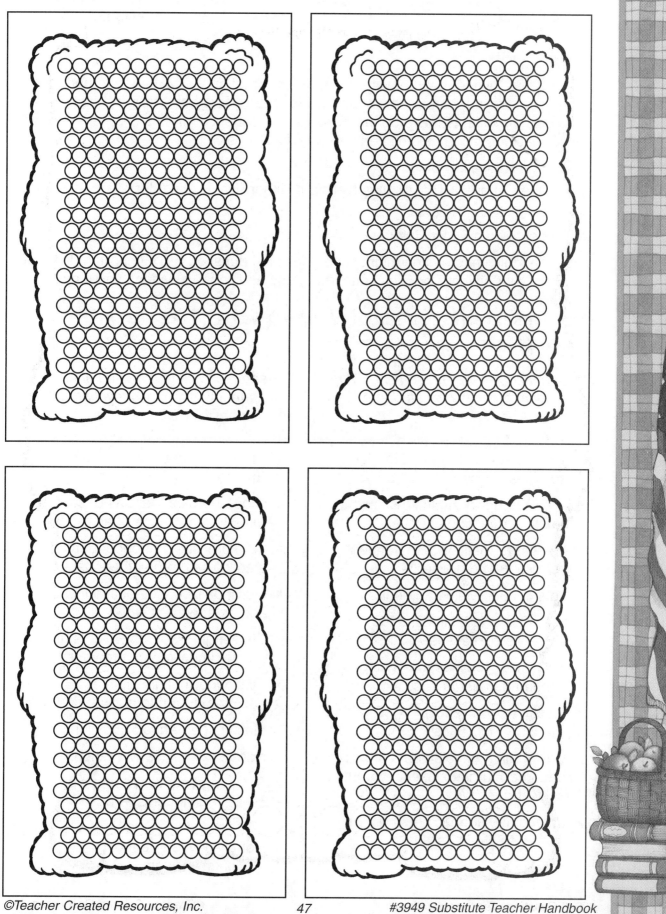

Chapter 3
Working with Special Populations

Introduction

Chapter 3 is a "hybrid" chapter with important information you will need to understand at some point in your career as a substitute teacher. More and more, special populations of students make up the classroom experience. In this chapter you will find information concerning children with special needs:

- ❖ Special-Education Students
- ❖ Children with ADHD (Attention Deficient Hypertension Disorder)
- ❖ High-Achieving Students
- ❖ Students from Other Cultures

As you read this chapter, you might have additional questions. It's important that you investigate your district's policies concerning any additional questions you may have.

What Research Says About Working with Students with Special Needs

*Research shows that these things **Will Help** low-academic-level students achieve basic skills.*	*Research shows that these things **Will Not Help** low-academic-level students achieve basic skills.*
✓ Time spent in structured learning activities led by the teacher.	✗ Time spent in unstructured or free time.
✓ Breaking down the instruction into small, sequenced activities.	✗ Long unbroken periods of seat work with student choice of activities.
✓ Plenty of repetition with frequent correction and praise.	✗ Little practice or independent practice with prompt feedback.
✓ Lots of supervision and help.	✗ Individualized, self-paced instruction and independent work.
✓ Materials or questions at the student's success level.	✗ Challenging work in which student will not know most of the answers.
✓ Many opportunities and much encouragement to succeed.	✗ Few opportunities or little encouragement to answer correctly.
✓ Mostly narrow teacher questions with one "right" answer.	✗ Mostly open-ended questions.
✓ Calling on non-volunteers or using patterned turns to select students to answer questions.	✗ Non-academic conversation.
✓ Immediate feedback (as right or wrong) to students' answers.	✗ Selecting only volunteers when calling on students to answer questions.
	✗ Not giving clear feedback to students' answers.

Working with Students Who Have Special Needs

It's estimated that 20% of students have one or more developmental, learning, or behavioral disorders. This means you will need to adjust your teaching practice.

How do I get them started?

Let these students know when you are starting and how long they will probably take to do the task. If possible, stay with them until they finish that initial stage of "I can't do this" or "Why do I have to do this—it's stupid." If the whole thing is daunting for them, break it into small parts.

How do I get them to stay on task?

Clear away as many distractions as possible. Be sure to clean off the desk. Sometimes a student like this actually performs better with a rubber ball to hold. Their tension goes directly into that object. Have another student nearby to tap on the desk when the special-needs student gets off task. Keep telling the student what a nice job he or she is doing.

How do I get them to stay in their seats?

Make sure your student knows what you expect. This type of child may feel a great need to get up and walk around for a little while. Use this as a reward after a set amount of time following directions. Keep them away from areas of distraction like the door, pencil sharpener, or drinking fountain.

How do I get them to follow directions?

This child doesn't understand or register subtle hints. You must be direct and clear in as few words as possible. Have the child repeat and explain what he or she is supposed to do. You may also have to go so far as to role-play the direction.

Classroom Strategies for ADHD

Environmental Interventions

1. Make sure this student knows what is expected.
2. Sit this student near the teacher.
3. Try using a carousel or separate seating.
4. Surround the child with others who know how to do the work.
5. Divide the workload into small, manageable "chunks."
6. Be very structured and consistent.
7. Allow for extra time when needed

Interpersonal Interventions

1. Understand what this child is capable of doing.
2. Connect briefly with the child during the day.
3. Give constant feedback.
4. Meet with the child one-on-one during the school year.
5. Give immediate rewards.
6. Give a lot of encouragement and praise.
7. Keep a log on this student's behavior, good and bad.
8. Help student to expand his or her attention span.
9. Teach the student to ask for help when confused.
10. Recognize the child's strengths and successes.
11. Look at the student often during the lesson.
12. Remember to use different modalities during your lesson.
13. Ask the student to repeat the instructions.
14. Make a plan for organizing the student.
15. Allow the student to stretch or take a break when needed.
16. Let the child know when a transition is coming.
17. Enforce rules and consequences immediately.
18. Redirect privately.

13 Major Diagnostic Signs of ADHD/ADD

If a child exhibits eight (8) or more of these signs, it is likely that attention disorder is related to the observed behaviors.

1. Often moves his or her feet or hands, or squirms in seat.
2. Has a real need to get up and move.
3. Anything seems to distract this student.
4. Has a very hard time waiting for his or her turn.
5. Wants to give answers or comments immediately without thinking them through.
6. Has trouble doing what others tell him or her to do.
7. Has difficulty sustaining attention in tasks or play activities.
8. Often goes to other tasks even before the first one is finished.
9. Talks a lot.
10. Interrupts others or takes things from other children.
11. Doesn't seem to hear you or pay attention when you talk to him or her.
12. Often loses things needed for school.
13. Often engages in dangerous activities without considering the consequences.

Modifying the Classroom Environment

The following are some key ways to modify the classroom environment for ADHD/ADD students. (See page 52 for a full checklist.)

- Learn to realize what this student can and should be expected to do.
- Change teaching strategies during the lesson.
- Create contracts with specific behaviors.
- Reward often and be able to change rewards every few weeks.
- Give this person a place to work apart from others.
- Allow this person some latitude in his or her responses.
- Use specific consequences.
- Give as much structure and consistency as possible.

Classroom Modifications for Special Needs Students

Teacher Checklist

- ❏ Reduce the number of assignments.

- ❏ Decrease the amount of writing in an assignment.

- ❏ Modify tests (e.g., read math problems to student).

- ❏ Extend time for assignment completion.

- ❏ Participation at homework center.

- ❏ Use a timer to determine the amount of time to be spent on a particular assignment.

- ❏ Use visual aids when giving instruction.

- ❏ Use short, concise directions.

- ❏ Have a buddy repeat the directions to the student.

- ❏ Student uses a personal chalkboard/whiteboard.

- ❏ Provide a special study area.

- ❏ Change cooperative group.

- ❏ Provide a special learning partner.

- ❏ Have the student use a notebook/contract for organization.

- ❏ Demand an organized desk area and notebook.

- ❏ Timeout to another classroom.

- ❏ Provide "activity breaks."

- ❏ Have the student dictate thought or story to an aide. Aide writes it down and student copies it.

- ❏ Encourage student to use a marker while reading.

- ❏ Change seating.

- ❏ Put fewer problems on each page.

- ❏ Assign short period of concentrated effort.

- ❏ Shorten assignments.

- ❏ Provide student with the opportunity to take the assignment home or to the homework center.

- ❏ Provide written directions.

- ❏ Encourage student to repeat your question before answering it.

- ❏ Teacher lists assignment on board and student copies it.

- ❏ Break complex directions into one- or two-step tasks.

- ❏ Change class assignments.

- ❏ Allow student to use earphones to screen out distractions while involved in a paper and pencil task.

- ❏ Put a hand on the student's arm or shoulder to gain and maintain attention for orally-presented materials.

- ❏ Vary test format.

- ❏ Deploy the student within classroom.

- ❏ Have the student work with an aide or cross-age tutor

- ❏ Have the student use a computer for writing assignments.

Resource List For Special Education

Books and Workbooks

Most of the following are available at major online bookstores:

Fay, J., & Funk, D. *Teaching with Love and Logic: Taking Control of the Classroom.* Love & Logic Press, 1995.

Flick, G. *ADD/ADHD Behavior-Change Resource Kit.* The Center for Applied Research in Education, 1998.

————. *How to Reach and Teach Teenagers with ADHD: A Step-By-Step Guide to Overcoming Difficult Behaviors at School and at Home.* The Center for Applied Research in Education, 2000.

Kindlon, D. & Thompson, M. *Raising Cain: Protecting the Emotional Lives of Boys.* Ballantine, 1999.

Maurice, C. *Behavioral Interventions for Young Children with Autism.* Pro-Ed., 1996.

Web Resources

Learning Disabilities

❖ *www.ldonline.org*
Click on "For Teachers."

❖ *www.ldresources.com*
Click on "Reading Writing & Learning."

Behavior Disorders

❖ *www.ccbd.net*
Click on "Teacher Resources."

❖ *www.as.wvu.edu/~scidis/behavior.html*
Click on "Introduction."

ADD/ADHD

❖ *www.adhd.com*
Click on "Educational Resources."

❖ *www.chadd.org*
Children & Adults with ADD.

❖ *www.newideas.net*
Click on "Teacher Resources."

❖ *www.understandingadhd.com*
Click on "Helping Kids with ADHD Succeed in School.

Glossary of Special-Education Terms

Adaptive Development

Describes how well the child is adapting in comparison to his or her peers.

Adaptive Physical Education (APE)

A special education service of developmental activities, games, sports, and rhythms suited to the abilities of the student. A child must qualify for this extra program.

Advocate

A person who works on behalf of a student or his/her family seeking special services from a school district.

Amendment

Any written change to a student's educational program.

Appropriate

Finding out what is suitable or proper for a student. This usually means the more typical situation.

Assessment

Usually a battery of tests that helps the school better understand the abilities and limitations of the student.

Assessment Team

The group of people who do the assessment.

At Risk

A label for children who are at risk of academic failure in the future.

Auditory Processing

How well we are able to process and learn from sounds.

Autism

A disability characterized by severe language and communication deficits, lack of normal relatedness, bizarre movement and self-stimulatory patterns, lack of normal handling of toys and other objects, and lack of most normal functional skills.

Glossary of Special-Education Terms *(cont.)*

Behavior Disorder

A behavior pattern that hinders the child from learning or from getting along with others.

Cognitive

Thinking, reasoning, understanding, and/or the ability to do these things.

Community Mental Health Services (CMHS)

The agency designated to provide mental-health assessment and services to students with special needs.

Compliance

Following the letter of the law when testing, evaluating, or offering services to a student.

Developmental

How well a person is going through the normal steps of maturity.

Developmental Tests

A given test that measures how well a child is developing in comparison with his or her peers.

Developmentally Delayed (DD)

When a child isn't able to process information or do tasks as well as his or her general population of peers.

Disability

The result of any physical or mental condition that affects or prevents one's ability to develop, achieve, and/or function in an educational setting at a normal rate.

Due Process (procedure)

An action that is designed to instill or protect the legal rights of a student or his or her family.

Early Intervention Services

Educational programs designed to create a learning experience for pre-school children.

Glossary of Special-Education Terms *(cont.)*

Educable Mentally Handicapped (EMH)

A disability; having a mild delay in the ability to learn and to function independently in the everyday environment. (A mild delay is defined as a rate of development and learning that is 50% to 75% of what is expected of a person the same age.)

Evaluation

The procedures used to determine if a child is eligible for early intervention services or whether a child has a disability and the type and extent of the special education that he or she qualifies to receive.

Extended School Year (ESY)

Longer school year—usually summer school for special-education students.

Fair Hearing

See "Due Process."

Free Appropriate Public Education (often referred to as FAPE)

Free education in the most "normal" setting available.

Gifted and Talented Education (GATE)

Provides special learning opportunities for students who have above-average intelligence in certain areas.

Guidance

Also known as "counseling."

Handicap

See "Disability."

Hearing Handicap/Hearing Impairment (HH)

A disability; a hearing loss that interferes with the ability to understand or use language and that affects learning in school.

Heterogeneous Classroom

A class where children might have similar educational needs but not the same disabilities.

Homogeneous Classroom

A grouping of children with similar disabilities.

Glossary of Special-Education Terms *(cont.)*

Individualized Education Program (IEP)

A written plan for a child with disabilities that describes the child's learning and educational needs and what educational goals will be set for the child.

Language Delay

When a child doesn't learn to use language at the same pace as his or her peers.

Learning Disability (LD)

See "Disability."

Learning Handicapped (LH)

A disability; the student's performance in the regular education classroom is well below expected levels.

Least Restrictive Environment (LRE)

A term that means the child should have the most interaction with regular education students possible. Most of the time this results in a pullout program that takes him/her out of the classroom for a short period of time.

Limited English Proficiency (LEP)

Refers to students whose primary language is other than English.

Mainstreaming

A term referring to the practice of putting the special-education student in a regular-education classroom for interaction with students there.

Mediation

If the school and parent cannot agree on a program for the child, they will hold this informal meeting with an impartial third party.

Moderately Mentally Disabled

Defined as a rate of development and learning 25% to 50% of what is expected of a child the same age.

Occupational Therapy

Treatment or training that helps an individual to develop physical skills that will aid in daily living, such as balance and coordination of movement, dressing, or eating with a utensil. This help is given when the problem interferes with the educational process.

Glossary of Special-Education Terms *(cont.)*

Placement

Once an IEP is written, the committee will decide where the student will best be served (e.g., SDC, Resource, etc.).

Program(s)

This is a placement for the sake of the special-education student that best meets his or her needs.

Referral

The request usually made by the parent or teacher have a child tested for possible special-education needs.

Related Services

Other services that a child with disabilities may require, such as speech and audiology, psychological services, physical and occupational therapy, recreation, counseling services, interpreters for the hearing impaired, and medical services.

Resource Specialist Program (RSP)

Students who are typically pulled out of the regular classroom setting for small-group or individual help.

Reverse Mainstreaming

When regular education children go to the special-education classroom to play and learn with children who are disabled.

Seriously Emotionally Disturbed (SED)

This disability prevents learning or getting along with other people.

Severely Handicapped (SH)

A disability category containing the currently used labels of trainable mentally handicapped, severely/profoundly handicapped, severely emotionally disturbed, autistic, and multi-handicapped.

Severely/Profoundly Handicapped (SPH)

A disability; having a very severe delay in the ability to learn and to function independently in the everyday environment. (A severe delay is defined as a rate of development and learning that is below 25% of what is expected of a person the same age.)

Glossary of Special-
Education Terms *(cont.)*

Special Day Class (SDC)

A self-contained classroom in which only students who require special-education instruction for more than 50% of the school day are enrolled.

Special Education (Sp. Ed.)

Specially-designed instruction, at no cost to the parents, to meet the unique needs of an eligible individual regardless of the nature or severity of their educational needs.

Special Needs (as in "special-needs child")

A term to describe a child who has disabilities or who is at risk of developing disabilities and requires special services or treatment in order to progress.

Student Study Team (SST)

A regular education process designed to make preliminary modifications within the regular education program of a student not succeeding in class.

Timeline

Also, "time limit."

Transition

Commonly used to refer to the change from secondary school to post-secondary programs, work, and independent living typical of young adults. Also used to describe other periods of major change, such as from early childhood to school or from more specialized to mainstreamed settings.

Visually Handicapped/Visually Disabled/Visually Impaired (VH)

A disability; a vision loss affecting the student's ability to learn.

Vocational Education (Voc Ed)

Education beginning in middle school through age 21, in which special education students participate in an adequately and appropriately supported work model that will include off-site job training, travel training, stranger training, social interaction, time management, and communication skills.

Activities for Gifted and High-Achieving Students

Story Starters

All these creative-writing topics emphasize the use of the upper levels of Bloom's Taxonomy. Again, it is not only gifted students who will benefit from activities like these. They are enjoyable activities for everyone, and they stimulate the higher-order thinking skills in everyone.

> **Note:** Teachers with gifted children in their classrooms need to pay particular attention to developing the upper three levels of Bloom's Taxonomy.
>
> ❖ **Synthesis**   ❖ **Evaluation**   ❖ **Analysis**

- Tell how to make a paper airplane (or anything else that is relatively simple to do).

- Describe an object without naming it.

- Write down all the actions of someone or something in the room.

- Pretend you are a tetherball (or anything else). Describe your feelings during the day.

- Describe a day in the life of a pencil. (Other nouns can be used.)

- Write a fairy tale in modern or futuristic terms.

- Invent a new machine; describe it.

- What would you put in a time capsule, and why?

- Invent a new holiday and tell how it came to be and how it will be celebrated.

- Write an advertisement for a make-believe product.

- Imagine the history of a discarded item in the junk pile.

- Invent a new vitamin.

- Re-design a piece of clothing you're wearing and describe it.

- Rewrite your favorite nursery rhyme and substitute slang words.

- Analyze the qualities of a superhero.

Activities for Gifted and High-Achieving Students (cont.)

Story Starters (cont.)

- Classify yourself as a car (or any object) and describe your parts accordingly.

- Analyze what you would do if you were lost in the woods with nothing but the clothes you're wearing, a pocket knife, and a match.

- Write down a conversation between a cat and a dog (or any two people or animals).

- How are your parents the same as and different from you?

- Discuss the differences between cars and oranges (any two items can be substituted).

- Analyze the construction of a chair.

- Describe the special abilities that a ballet dancer needs. (Other nouns can be substituted.)

- Describe the actions of an ant you are observing. (Other animals can be substituted.)

- How does it feel to look down from a high place (or from any precarious position)?

- Describe a meeting between your teacher and Superman (or any unlikely combination of two people).

- Critique your favorite TV show.

- Recommend three things that will be essential for those living 25 years from now.

- Debate an issue (handguns, smoking in public places, etc.) by writing the pros and cons.

- Write a note to put in a satellite to tell how good or bad Earth is.

- Is it a good idea to tell a secret? Why or why not?

- What is the most perfect place to be?

- What is the "good life"?

- What does generosity mean?

- Defend the idea that Earth is round.

- Describe your house from a visitor's point of view.

Activities for Gifted and High-Achieving Students *(cont.)*

Activity Cards

Listed below are a number of popular activities to use with stories. On the surface they may appear to be fun and games; in actuality, they utilize upper-level thinking skills.

Play Write and perform a play based on the story.	**Diary** Write a diary for one of the characters telling what happened to him or her.
Pantomime Pantomime the story (or your favorite part of the story).	**Time Line** Make a time line of the events of the story. Explain it.
TV Commercial Write and perform a TV commercial to sell the book.	**Dress-Up** Dress up like one of the characters and tell what happened to him or her.
Comic Book Make a comic book based on the book.	**Listening Post** Listen to students reading favorite parts of the book.
Book Cover Create a book cover for the story. Explain it.	**Drawings** Make a series of five drawings depicting the major points. Describe them.

Activities for Gifted and
High-Achieving Students (cont.)

Activity Cards (cont.)

Read/Record

Tape-record the story (or favorite part of the book) in your best reading voice. Add sound effects.

New Character

Create another character for the story. Tell how things would change with this character's presence.

Author Biography

Research and prepare an oral report on the author's life.

Rewrite Story

Rewrite your favorite part of the book. Use yourself as a character and a favorite place as the setting.

Filmstrip

Create a filmstrip of the story. Describe each frame as you show it.

Roll Movie

Draw a series of pictures depicting events in the books and an example of each on shelf paper. Make a "roll movie" of the story. Explain the story as you show it.

Book Display

Put together a display of other books the author has written. Tell about them.

Radio Advertisement

Write and tape-record a radio advertisement that will make people want to read the story.

New Ending

Create a new ending for the story. Explain why it is better than the original.

Quilt

Make a friendship quilt of the story. Each student sews or draws a square depicting an incident from the book. As a class, sequence them together into a quilt.

Activities for Gifted and High-Achieving Students *(cont.)*

Activity Cards *(cont.)*

Poster Create a poster advertising the book. Explain it.	**Ten Questions** Play this game with others: Ask 10 questions about a character in the book. By the end of the tenth question or before, they should guess the character.
Crossword Puzzle Construct a crossword puzzle of words and their definitions from the story.	**To Read/Not to Read** Students give reasons to read and not to read the book.
Poem Write and illustrate a poem about the story.	**Puppet Show** Perform a puppet show of the story.
Bumper Sticker Make a bumper sticker advertising the story.	**Newspaper** Design the front page of a newspaper with headlines and a story about what happened in the book.
Movie Poster Draw a movie poster advertising the story, and cast a real actor in each character's role. Explain it.	**Model** Construct a model of something used in the book. Describe it.

Working with Other Cultures

Consider the cultural differences before engaging in any of the following:

- Appropriateness of using telephone to communicate with parents

- Patting a child on the head as a sign of affection

- Expecting children to look you in the eye when being scolded

- Looking people you've just met in the eye when simply talking

- Shaking hands, pointing, gesturing "come"

- Being informal vs. courteous (e.g., it's better to overdress than underdress)

- Asking them their preferences and explaining your behavior

Ways Teachers Can Make a World of Difference

- ❖ First of all, **Do No Harm!**

- ❖ Be respectful and respectable.

- ❖ Be inviting and caring.

- ❖ Give the benefit of the doubt when your "cultural" feelings are hurt.

- ❖ Be flexible with plenty of wait time.

- ❖ Try more to understand than be understood, then teach and explain.

- ❖ Be hypercritical, not hypocritical, of your own behavior!

Working with Other Cultures (cont.)

Multicultural Education Isn't	Multicultural Education Is
✗ About everyone agreeing and getting along	✓ About naming and eliminating the inequities in education
✗ Only applicable to Language Arts and History	✓ A comprehensive approach for making education more inclusive, active, and engaging in all subject areas
✗ A process of watering down good curriculum	✓ A process for presenting all students with a more comprehensive, accurate understanding of the world
✗ Related only to curriculum reform	✓ Related to all aspects of education, including pedagogy, counseling, administration, assessment and evaluation, research, etc.
✗ Only for teachers and students of color	
✗ Achieved through a series of small changes	✓ For all students and educators
✗ Modeled through cultural bulletin boards, assemblies, or fairs	✓ Achieved through the re-examination and transformation of all aspects of education
✗ The responsibility of culture-based student clubs or organizations	✓ Modeled through self-critique, self-examination, and cross-cultural relationship-building
✗ A single in-service workshop	✓ The responsibility of teachers, administrators, and school staff

Used with permission from *Strategies for Choosing and Using Activities and Exercises for Intergroup Learning* by Paul Gorski.

Working with Other Cultures (cont.)

When Using Multicultural Activities . . .

- ❑ Be able to change the type of activities and exercises you use. Possible examples are whole class or large group, small groups, or partner share; simulations; role play; narrative; storytelling; and project making.

- ❑ Have plenty of time for the students to dialogue and process.

- ❑ Always start your lesson plan with concepts, and then add activities—never the reverse.

- ❑ Whenever possible and appropriate, show the students you are willing to participate in the class exercises and activities. This gives strength to the position that everyone can share.

- ❑ Role-playing is good, but it also needs to be balanced with real personal experiences followed by discussions.

- ❑ Films can provide excellent illustration of concepts and lead to fruitful dialogues, but they should be short enough to allow for class dialogue.

- ❑ Be creative. Too often, educators and facilitators become dependent on one or two activities or exercises. Canned activities and exercises are not designed to be used for every situation. After you've done it enough, you will have a sense for what will and will not work within that context.

Adapted and used with permission from *Strategies for Choosing and Using Activities and Exercises for Intergroup Learning* by Paul Gorski.

Culture Shock

Understanding the Condition

The term "culture shock" was introduced for the first time in 1958 to describe the anxiety produced when a person moves to a completely new environment. This term expresses the feeling of not knowing what or how to do things in a new environment, of not knowing what is appropriate or inappropriate. The feeling of culture shock generally sets in after the first few weeks of coming to a new place.

We can describe culture shock as the physical and emotional discomfort one suffers when coming to live in another country or a place different from one's place of origin. Often, the way that we lived before is not accepted or considered normal in the new place. Everything is different—the language, not knowing how to use banking machines, not knowing how to use the telephone, and so forth.

The symptoms of cultural shock can appear at different times. Although one can experience real pain from culture shock, it is also an opportunity for redefining one's life objectives. It is a great opportunity for learning and acquiring new perspectives. Culture shock can make one develop a better understanding of oneself and stimulate personal creativity.

Symptoms

- ❖ Sadness, loneliness, melancholy
- ❖ Preoccupation with health
- ❖ Aches, pains, and allergies
- ❖ Insomnia, desire to sleep too much or too little
- ❖ Changes in temperament, depression, feeling vulnerable, feeling powerless
- ❖ Anger, irritability, resentment, unwillingness to interact with others
- ❖ Identifying with the old culture or idealizing the old country
- ❖ Loss of identity
- ❖ Trying too hard to absorb everything in the new culture or country
- ❖ Unable to solve simple problems
- ❖ Lack of confidence
- ❖ Feelings of inadequacy or insecurity
- ❖ Developing stereotypes about the new culture
- ❖ Developing obsessions, such as over-cleanliness
- ❖ Longing for family
- ❖ Feelings of being lost, overlooked, exploited, or abused

68

Culture Shock (cont.)

Stages of Culture Shock

Culture shock has many stages. Each stage can be ongoing or appear only at certain times. The first stage is the incubation stage. In this first stage, the new arrival may feel euphoric and be pleased by all of the new things encountered. This time is called the "honeymoon" stage, as everything encountered is new and exciting.

Afterwards, the second stage presents itself. A person may encounter some difficult times and crises in daily life. For example, communication difficulties may occur, such as not being understood. In this stage, there may be feelings of discontent, impatience, anger, sadness, and incompetence. This happens when a person is trying to adapt to a new culture that is very different from their culture of origin. Transition between the old methods and those of the new country is a difficult process and takes time to complete. During the transition, there can be strong feelings of dissatisfaction.

The third stage is characterized by gaining some understanding of the new culture. A new feeling of pleasure and sense of humor may be experienced. One may start to feel a certain psychological balance. The new arrival may not feel as lost and starts to have a feeling of direction. The individual is more familiar with the environment and wants to belong. This initiates an evaluation of the old ways versus the new.

In the fourth stage, the person realizes that the new culture has good and bad things to offer. This stage can be one of double integration or triple integration depending on the number of cultures that the person has to process. This integration is accompanied by a more solid feeling of belonging. The person starts to define him/herself and establish goals for living.

The fifth stage is the stage that is called the "re-entry shock." This occurs upon a return to the country of origin. One may find that things are no longer the same—for example, some of the newly-acquired customs are not in use in the old culture.

These stages are present at different times, and each person has his or her own way of reacting to the stages of culture shock. As a consequence, some stages will be longer and more difficult than others. Many factors contribute to the duration and effects of culture shock. For example, the individual's state of mental health, type of personality, previous experiences, socio-economic conditions, familiarity with the language, family and/or social support systems, and level of education can all contribute to the severity of culture shock.

> Adapted and used with permission from "Culture Shock" by Dr. Carmen Guanipa, Dept. of Counseling and School Psychology, San Diego State University.

Collaborative Multicultural Problem-Solving

1. Problem Identification

Identify or name the situation and relevant related issues. What is the conflict? What is the source of the conflict?

2. Perspectives

Create a list of every person, group, and institution affected by the incident. How are each of these people and institutions affected by the situation? Be sure to include possible victims, victimizers, members of the community, and anyone else who is touched by the incident, directly or indirectly. It may be necessary to make some assumptions for this step, intensifying the importance of incorporating as many voices and perspectives as possible into the process of compiling the information.

3. Challenges and Opportunities

With the varied perspectives in mind, what will be the individual and institutional challenges and constraints to addressing the situation? What will be the challenges based on the individuals directly involved, and what institutional constraints must inform an approach for addressing the situation? What are the educational opportunities presented by the incident, both for the people directly involved and everyone else?

4. Strategies

Brainstorm ways to address the situation, attempting to maximize the extent to which the negative outcomes of the situation are addressed while maximizing the extent to which you take advantage of educational opportunities. Keep in mind the varied perspectives and the fact that any solution will affect everyone differently. This is not the step at which to challenge and critique each other's ideas. Record every idea, no matter how unreasonable it may sound to individuals in the group.

5. Solutions

Focus your strategies into a formal plan of action. Keep in mind the varied perspectives, as well as the challenges and opportunities. Be sure to come up with at least two or three specific responses, whether they focus on the individual conflict or the underlying issues at an institutional level.

6. Expected Outcomes

Name the outcomes you foresee as a result of the solutions you identified. Revisit the perspectives step to ensure a standard of equity and fairness.

Permission Note: This model was created in 2000 and revised in 2001 by Paul Gorski. See permission on pp. 66 and 67.

English/Spanish
Reinforcement Statements

English	Español
Ann is paying attention.	Ana está poniendó attentión.
It looks like you put a lot of work into this.	Parece que mucho esfuerzo en esto.
Very creative.	Muy creativo(a).
Very interesting.	Muy interesante.
Good thinking.	Buena idea.
That's an interesting way of looking at it.	Esa es una manera interesante de verlo.
Now you've figured it out.	Ya lo has resuelto ahora.
Clifford has it.	Clifford lo tiene.
That's the right answer.	Esa es la contestación correcta.
Now you've got the hang of it.	Ahora ya lo has entendido.
Exactly right.	Perfectamente correcto.
Super!	¡Magnífico!
Superior work.	Un trabajo excelente.
That's a good point.	Ese es un buen punto.
That's a very good observation.	Esa es una buena observación.
That certainly is one way of looking at it.	Esa es ciertamente una manera de verlo.
That's an interesting point of view.	Ese es un punto de vista muy interesante.
Thank you for raising your hand, Charles.	Gracias por lavantar la mano, Charles.
What is it?	¿Qué pasa?
You've got it now.	Ya lo entendiste ahora.
Out of sight!	¡Qué manera de hacerlo!
Nice going.	Buena conducta. Buen proceder.
Fantastic!	¡Fantástico!
You make it look easy.	Tú (Uds.) lo hacen ver fácil.
That's coming along nicely.	Eso está resultando muy bien.
You've got it made!	¡Te viene tan fácil!
Super!	¡Estupendo!
That's right!	¡Correcto!

English/Spanish
Reinforcement Statements (cont.)

English	Español
That's good!	¡Qué bien!
You are very good at that.	Tu eres magnifica para eso.
Good work!	¡Buen trabajo!
Exactly right!	¡Exacto!
You've just about got it.	Ya casi lo tienes.
You are doing a good job.	Estás haciendo buen trabajo.
That's it!	¡Eso es!
Now you've figured it out.	Ya lo figuraste.
I knew you could do it.	Yo sabia que lo podias hacer.
Great!	¡Fantastico!
Congratulations!	¡Felicitaciones!
Not bad.	No está mal.
Now you have it.	Ya aprendiste.
Keep working on it; you're improving.	Continúa, estás mejorando.
You are learning fast.	Al fin aprendiste. Estas aprendiendo rapido.
Good for you!	¡Qué bueno!
Couldn't have done it better myself.	Yo no hubiera podido hacerlo mejor.
Beautiful!	¡Lindo! ¡Que bonito!
One more time and you'll have it.	Una vez más y ya lo tienes.
That's the right way to do it.	Es la única forma de hacerlo.
You did it that time!	¡Lograste hacerlo esa vez!
You're getting better and better.	Vas mejorando cada vez más.
You're on the right track now.	Estás en buen camino (o bien encaminado).
Nice going.	Vas bien.
You haven't missed a thing.	Lo has hecho a la perfección.
That's the way.	Asi se hace.
Keep up the good work.	Sigue con el buen trabajo.

English/Spanish
Reinforcement Statements *(cont.)*

English	Español
Terrific!	¡Estupendo!
Nothing can stop you now.	Ahora nada puede cruzarse en tu camino.
That's the way to do it.	Esa es la manera de hacerlo.
Sensational!	¡Sensacional!
You've got your brain in gear today.	Hoy funciona tu cerebro.
That's better.	Así es mejor.
Excellent!	¡Excelente!
That was first-class work.	Hiciste trabajo de primera clase.
That's the best ever.	Lo mejor que has hecho.
You've just about mastered that.	Ya lo tienes bajo control.
Perfect!	¡Perfecto!
That's better than ever.	¡Mejor que nunca!
Much better!	¡Mucho mejor!
Wonderful!	¡Magnifico!
You must have been practicing!	¡Debes haber estado practicando!
You did that very well.	Lo hiciste muy bien.
Fine!	¡Que bien!
Nice going.	Asi se hace.
Outstanding!	¡Sobresaliente!
Fabulous!	¡Fabuloso!
Now that's what I call a fine job!	¡Eso es lo que se llama un buen trabajo!
That's great!	¡Admirable!
You're really improving.	Realmente estás mejorando.
Superb!	¡Soberbio!
Good remembering!	¡Buena memoria!
You've got that down pat!	¡Ya lo aprendiste bien!
You certainly did well today.	En realidad estuviste muy bien hoy.

Chapter 4
Strategies for Teaching

Introduction

There isn't any easy way to say it but to just say it: there are times when even the best veteran teacher has a hard time keeping the lesson going. You are definitely going to have this happen to you, because teaching from someone else's plans is difficult. Relying on someone else who isn't in the class is a hard trick to pull off. This chapter is designed to do just that: give you strategies to use when a lesson isn't going well. Here you will find the following tricks of the trade:

- ❖ Brainstorming
- ❖ Concept Mapping
- ❖ K-W-L Charting
- ❖ Cooperative Learning
- ❖ Questioning Techniques
- ❖ General Strategies for All Learners
- ❖ Graphic Organizers
- ❖ Lesson Planning Ideas

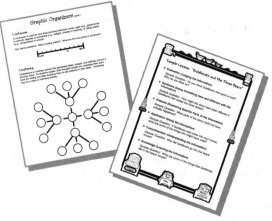

We want you to do more than just survive. Examine your relationship to the classroom. How can you affect classroom learning? What different techniques can you use? What have you seen that you think you could try?

Brainstorming

Brainstorming is a group technique for generating new, useful ideas and promoting creative thinking.

It can be used to help do the following:

- ✓ Define what project or problem you want to work on
- ✓ Diagnose problems
- ✓ Simplify a project by coming up with possible solutions.

An example of one classroom brainstorming activity might include having students list as many things as possible that they know about a farm. A possible time limit for generating ideas might be five minutes. Students' ideas could then be listed, discussed, and put into topics.

This is usually done as a whole class, with the teacher acting as the facilitator. If you want to do it with small groups, there are three roles the students should assume: leader, scribe, and team member.

Brainstorming (cont.)

The Problem Statement or Question

1. This needs to be something that the participants are familiar with and that is focused, yet open-ended.

2. It should not be something that is easily solved—for example, "What kind of animal lives in Africa and has an extremely long neck?"

Ground Rules for Brainstorming

✓ Students will not be allowed to judge other students' ideas.

✓ Students' ideas must be original.

✓ Generate as many ideas as possible.

✓ Team members must participate.

✓ Try to have as many good ideas as possible in a short period of time.

✓ Only one idea will be contributed each turn. A member may decline to contribute during a particular round, but will be asked to contribute each round.

✓ Participants should not provide explanations for ideas during brainstorming. Doing so would both slow the process down and allow premature evaluation of ideas.

Steps for the Leader on How to Brainstorm

1. Introduce the topic. Let everyone know the reason for the brainstorming session and discuss the ground rules.

2. Set a time limit of 20 to 25 minutes. Stop when you think the group is finished generating good ideas. It's best not to force the discussion. If someone other than the teacher is acting as the scribe, then that person must note all suggestions made and make the note just the way the speaker said it. The scribe may have to summarize the statement if it is too long.

3. Process the ideas. Look over each idea and make sure everyone understands what has been written. If you see some ideas that are similar, group them together.

4. Establish a consensus, if appropriate. Have the group vote on five ideas to consider.

Ideas . . . for Brainstorming Ideas

When writing with elementary-age students, it is good to first help them organize their thoughts by brainstorming. Here are some possible topics:

➥ What do you have to do to take care of your pet?

➥ What kinds of jobs require electricity?

➥ Describe a friend.

Concept Mapping

Concept mapping is a technique for representing knowledge in graphs. Graphs of this sort are a connection of ideas. Teachers begin by listing a main concept and branching related items to that thought. An example might look like this:

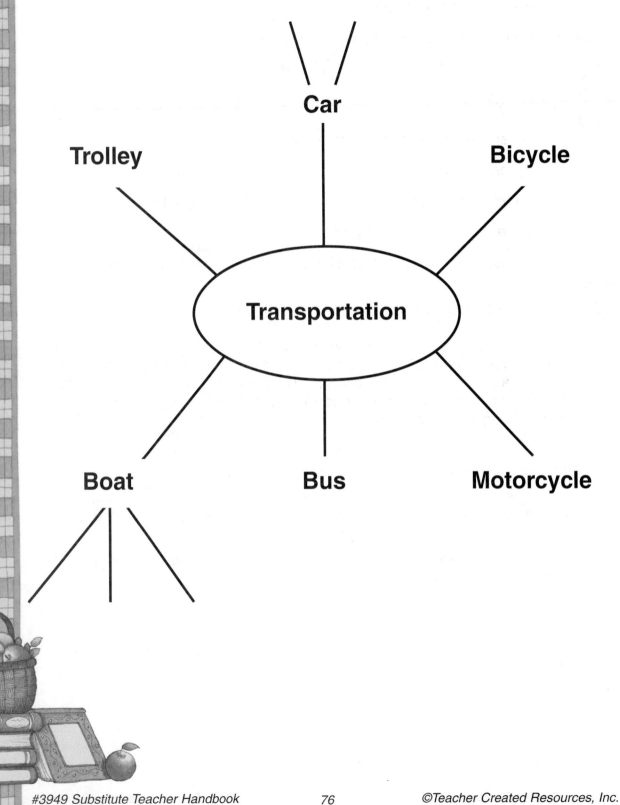

Concept Mapping *(cont.)*

 ## Here are some critical questions to ask when concept mapping:

- ❧ What is the central word, concept, research question, or problem around which to build the map?

- ❧ What are the concepts, items, descriptive words, or telling questions that you can associate with the concept, topic, research question, or problem?

 ## Concept mapping can be done for several purposes:

- ✓ To generate ideas (brainstorming, etc.)

- ✓ To design a class project

- ✓ To look at complex ideas

- ✓ To learn something new by looking at what the students already know

- ✓ To assess student understanding or diagnose misunderstanding.

 ## How do I use concept maps in my classroom?

Concept maps can be used in a variety of ways. They can be a kind of diary in the classroom, which can keep track of student progress over a period of time. Classroom discussions can be guided from this type of input, and the teacher may also structure lectures, discussions, and review sessions by constructing a concept map.

K-W-L Charting

This instructional technique calls for teachers to activate students' prior knowledge by asking them what they already **Know**; the students (collaborating as a classroom unit or within small groups) set goals specifying what they **Want to Know**; and after reading and engaging in educational activities, students discuss what they **Learned**. (See page 79 for a sample lesson that uses a K-W-L chart, and see page 80 for a blank K-W-L chart template.)

Teachers use information to compare, contrast, and discuss with students what they knew at first, what they learned, and if the students gained the knowledge they had hoped for. Students apply higher-order thinking strategies, which help them construct meaning from what they read and help them monitor their progress toward their goals.

- Give each child a K-W-L chart and allow about five minutes to fill out the first column. (Students will keep the chart in their folders, to add to or change during the unit of study.)

- As a class, fill in the **Know** column of a large, poster-sized K-W-L chart.

- Repeat the process for the **Want To Know** column.

- This chart can be an ongoing project throughout the unit. Give children the opportunity daily to write down what they have learned or to evaluate things they thought they **Knew**. Once a week, review the classroom chart, evaluating the items in the **What We Know** column, crossing out things they now know not to be true and adding items in the **What We Learned** column.

Key Terms to Know

Transfer—Relating learning to past and/or future learning to promote continuity and so that learning does not appear to be fragmented or random.

Objective—Calling students' attention to the intended learning outcomes, which will occur by the end of the lesson.

Modeling—The teacher shows the students how to do a skill. It is shown exactly as the children are expected to do it.

Sample K-W-L Chart Lesson

Lesson Procedure

Set/Initiation: Remind students that the class is going to read the book *Gentle Ben,* which is about a boy who has a pet bear. This book will help them understand more about this animal.

Main Activities:

1. For the pre-reading activity, fill out the "K" section on your K-W-L chart. Do this together. The teacher writes down the responses.
   - Ask students what they already know about bears.
   - What bears have they seen?
   - What would it be like to have a bear for a pet?

2. The teacher will now focus on key categories to be examined in the story. Ask the students to think about some questions they would like to have answered. The teacher then writes those questions down in the "W" column of the chart.
   - Do bears eat plants?
   - Do bears live around here?
   - Do bears sleep all winter?

3. After reading the story, it is time to ask the students the following questions:
   - What did you learn?
   - Did you find out what you wanted to know?
   - Was there anything not covered in the story?
   - Record all responses on the K-W-L Chart.

K What Do I Know?	W What I Want to Know?	L What I Learned?
• Bears are big and fierce. • Bears eat honey. • They climb trees. • They hibernate. • They scare me. • They are mammals.	• Do they eat plants? • Do they eat people? • Do they sleep all winter? • Do bears live around here? • What do you do if you see a bear?	• They wake up during their hibernation. • They eat plants and animals. • The biggest bear is the Alaskan brown bear.

K-W-L Chart

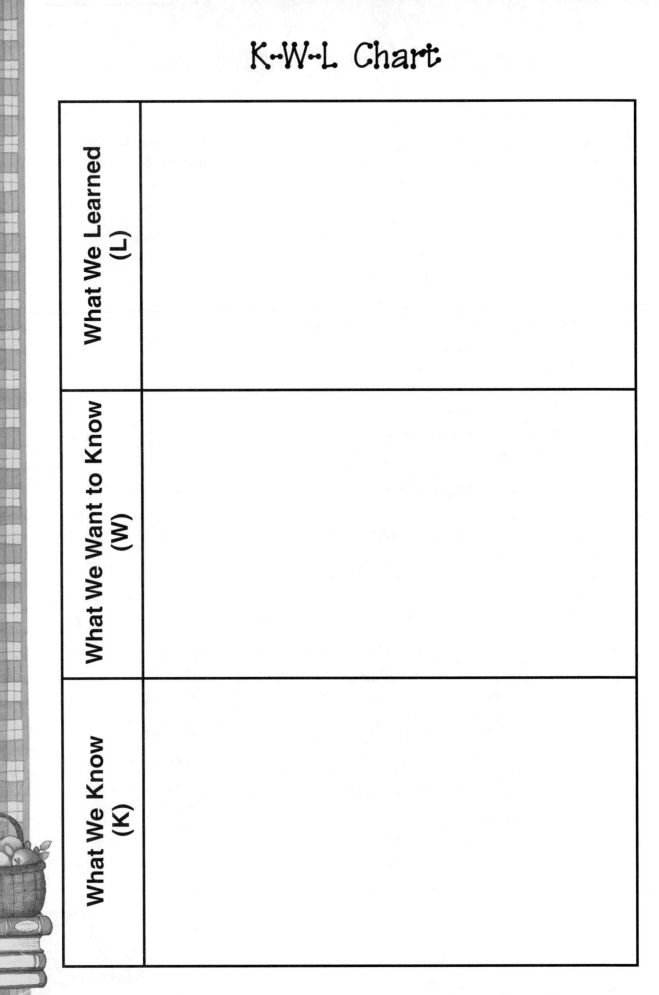

What We Know (K)	What We Want to Know (W)	What We Learned (L)

Cooperative Learning

The use of cooperative groups is one of the best-researched of all teaching strategies. It works because students learn faster and more efficiently, have greater retention, and feel more positive about their learning experiences when they work in groups. Unfortunately, like everything else we want students to learn, we have to teach them how to do this before we can expect any degree of success. You can't just put them in groups and tell them to work together to come up with something. If you do this, you'll be very disappointed with the end product.

Everyone has a role in this process. Even though the teacher isn't assigned to any one group, he or she has plenty to do.

 ## The teacher's role is as follows:

- ➨ Observe and intervene during in-class group work.

- ➨ Ask open-ended questions during group work.

- ➨ Praise and encourage during group work.

- ➨ Help students understand their role in the group.

- ➨ Supply all needed materials.

The students have very active roles in the learning, as well. They become peer experts and act as peer instructors. They are also responsible for each other and the group. They also may have an assigned role.

 ## The students' roles are as follows:

- ➨ The **team leader** or **coordinator** keeps people on track and may also be the presenter.

- ➨ The **recorder** writes down ideas.

- ➨ The **collector** makes sure the group has everything they need.

- ➨ The **checker** makes sure everyone is meeting their goals.

- ➨ The **sergeant-at-arms** makes sure everyone works well together.

See pages 82 and 83 for several useful partner strategies.

Partner Strategies

The use of partners is practically limitless. Using pairs is an excellent place to begin structured cooperation, increase participation, foster access for all students, develop language, and engage higher-order thinking. As with all cooperative-learning strategies, it is important for teachers to think through lesson goals, time constraints, and student needs to select the right partner strategy for the right place in the lesson. A few "tried and true" examples of partner strategies include the following:

Think, Pair, Share

When: before, during, and/or after instruction

- First pose a question, such as, "What do you predict the next chapter will probably tell us?"
- Then allow students to think quietly (and/or jot a few notes down).
- Have students work in pairs. They should share ideas with their partners (compare, contrast, consensus, etc.).
- Finally, have the pairs share with the class. This provides much richer discussions, and everyone is involved.

The key to "Think, Pair, Share" is the quality of the question. It works best if the question is a higher-level thought. Have students analyze, infer, compare, think of an example of, etc.

Variations: Combine journal/notebook writing with the "think" stage; do the pair work standing up (to get the body moving); combine partners to "square" or form teams of four to extend the discussion before the whole-class discussion.

Tell, Help, Check

When: During and/or after instruction

- This is a great review strategy for less prepared students. They need active review but are usually passive in class. This involves them immediately.
- Tell your partner the answer (no peeking!).
- Others, help your partner add to or expand on their answer. It's best to do this by assigning partners 1's & 2's (e.g., "1's tell 2's," etc.).
- Check your notes, book, overhead, etc., for the best answers.

Partner Reading

When: During instruction

- Students can keep the same roles or change at your discretion. It's usually best to have the more skilled reader read first.
    - 1's read a paragraph out loud, 2's follow along.
        - 2's respond by summarizing the key ideas, paraphrasing, predicting, etc.
            - Next, repeat, but change the roles this time.

Partner Strategies *(cont.)*

Think, Talk, Record, Share: Brainstorming

When: Before and/or after instruction

- This is a flexible brainstorming strategy that can be used with all ages. If writing is a problem, then skip the record step and just ask students to choose two or three favorites.
- Have students think about an issue or topic by asking a question, such as, "What do I know about Dinosaurs?"
- Have students talk with their partners to come up with all the possibilities.
- Have students write down their ideas. (Assign one student in each group to be the recorder. That student creates a list of the group's ideas.)
- Have students share their ideas with a larger group and/or with the whole class.

Do, Check, Teach

When: After instruction; independent work

- Have students do the problem/answer the question by themselves.
- They then need to check their answers with the key.
- If one partner misses the item, the other partner teaches the process, concept, etc.

Pairs Check

When: After instruction; independent work

- 1's do the item, while 2's coach and describe their thinking as they work.
- 2's check their partners' work for agreement. If they don't agree, they ask another pair on their team of four for the answer.
- 2's praise the work of their partners, then switch roles and repeat the steps.
- Teams of four get together. They check for agreement and figure out answers. They only ask for help if they're all stumped and can't agree.

Pairs Check is a very flexible strategy that is very helpful to students when they are practicing new skills or learning a new strategy. It is important to teach your students how to help one another. Model this for them and give lots of coaching feedback.

Teaching Partners

When: After instruction or during independent work

- I do it: As a model, have one student do one item for their partner.
- We do it: Partners do the item together.
- You do it: The partner does the item for the first student.

Three-Step Interview

When: Before and after instruction/activities

- 1's interview 2's for a certain number of minutes about a certain topic.
- Repeat the process with roles reversed.
- Share either in teams of four, one at a time, or as a whole class.

Questioning Techniques

<table>
<tr><td colspan="2" align="center">

Six Components of Bloom's Taxonomy
</td></tr>
<tr><td>

1. **Knowledge**
</td><td>

4. **Analysis**
</td></tr>
<tr><td>

2. **Comprehension**
</td><td>

5. **Synthesis**
</td></tr>
<tr><td>

3. **Application**
</td><td>

6. **Evaluation**
</td></tr>
</table>

☞ At least 90% of the questions that teachers ask of their students are from the lowest levels (Knowledge and Comprehension).

☞ Higher-level thinking questions need to be incorporated into the curriculum to meet the needs of all students (Synthesis and Evaluation).

☞ Students should be asked higher-level questions instead of the lower-level questions where they just parrot answers back to the teacher.

☞ We get from students what we ask of them. If we ask only the most basic of questions, we will get only the most basic of responses.

☞ Students are more engaged in learning when they are asked higher-level thinking questions.

☞ The level of questions that you ask will determine how effective your lesson is.

☞ Lower-level questions are embedded in the higher-level questions.

☞ We need to stretch the minds of children. We need to teach them how to think. We can do this by asking them higher-level-thinking questions.

☞ Encourage student question-asking behavior and peer questioning to improve student engagement and to probe for misunderstandings in their inquiry process.

See page 85 for a sample lesson that uses higher-level-questioning techniques. See pages 86 and 87 for more ways to apply Bloom's Taxonomy and higher-level-questioning techniques to your lessons.

Applying Bloom's Taxonomy

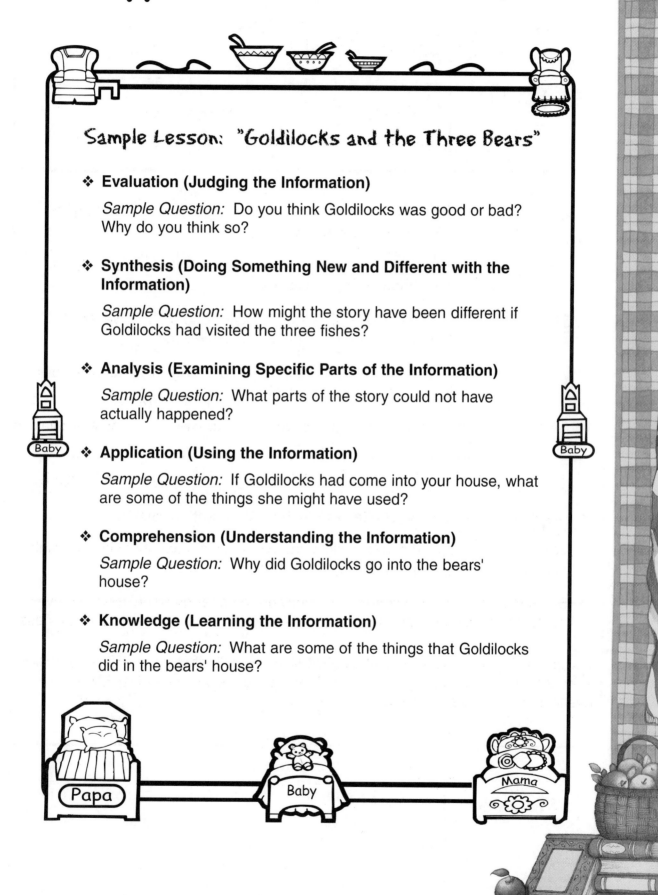

Sample Lesson: "Goldilocks and the Three Bears"

❖ **Evaluation (Judging the Information)**

Sample Question: Do you think Goldilocks was good or bad? Why do you think so?

❖ **Synthesis (Doing Something New and Different with the Information)**

Sample Question: How might the story have been different if Goldilocks had visited the three fishes?

❖ **Analysis (Examining Specific Parts of the Information)**

Sample Question: What parts of the story could not have actually happened?

❖ **Application (Using the Information)**

Sample Question: If Goldilocks had come into your house, what are some of the things she might have used?

❖ **Comprehension (Understanding the Information)**

Sample Question: Why did Goldilocks go into the bears' house?

❖ **Knowledge (Learning the Information)**

Sample Question: What are some of the things that Goldilocks did in the bears' house?

Bloom's Process Verbs

Synthesis	create suppose design organize	combine compose formulate construct	compile arrange prepare generate	draw assemble plan write	modify devise propose revise
Evaluation	justify value assess estimate	conclude choose compare	decide evaluate judge	summarize measure rate	select predict contrast
Analysis	categorize compare criticize experiment	separate differentiate select discriminate	analyze divide distinguish break down	outline diagram inventory	debate question point out
Application	use demonstrate illustrate prepare	discover schedule pretend change	compute interpret practice relate	solve dramatize apply	operate imply translate
Comprehension	tell explain locate paraphrase	infer review generalize give examples	extend summarize recognize	rewrite discuss report	restate express find
Knowledge	name repeat describe	recall state identify	list match relate	memorize label	define record

Taxonomy of Thinking

Category	Definition	Trigger Words	Products
Synthesis	Re-form individual parts to make a new whole	Compose, Design, Invent, Create, Hypothesize, Construct, Forecast, Rearrange parts, Imagine	Lesson Plan, Song, Poem, Story, Ad, Invention
Evaluation	Judge value of something vis-à-vis criteria Support judgment	Judge, Evaluate, Give opinion, Viewpoint, Prioritize, Recommend, Critique	Decision, Rating/Grades, Editorial, Debate, Critique, Defense/Verdict
Analysis	Understand how parts relate to a whole Understand structure and motive	Investigate, Classify, Categorize, Compare, Contrast, Solve	Survey, Questionnaire, Plan, Solution, Report, Prospectus
Application	Transfer knowledge learned in one situation to another	Demonstrate; Use guides, maps, charts, etc.; Build, Cook	Recipe, Model, Artwork, Demonstrate, Crafts
Comprehension	Demonstrate basic understanding of concepts and curriculum Translate to other words	Restate, Give examples, Explain, Summarize, Translate, Show symbols, Edit	Drawing, Diagram, Response to question, Revision
Knowledge	Ability to remember something previously learned	Tell, Recite, List, Memorize, Remember, Define, Locate	Workbook pages, Quiz, Test, Exam, Vocabulary, Facts in isolation

General Strategies
for All Learners

- ❑ Allow students more time to complete assignments.
- ❑ Shorten the length of assignments.
- ❑ Provide for more practice for over-learning.
- ❑ Time students as they complete assignments.
- ❑ Show the students how to arrange the paper in columns and rows.
- ❑ Break lessons into smaller parts for students experiencing difficulty.
- ❑ Use a multi-sensory approach.
- ❑ Teach to students' strengths.
- ❑ Use lots of visual aids.
- ❑ Monitor the pace of your presentations and vary it as necessary.
- ❑ Use concrete materials as much as possible.
- ❑ Focus on your students' interests.
- ❑ Use high-interest materials.
- ❑ Use brief and specific instructions, and have students repeat them.
- ❑ Use peer or cross-age tutors.
- ❑ Praise students for what they get right instead of focusing on what they missed.

Curriculum Design

Essential Questions for Planning

 What am I going to teach, and why?

❑ Long-term and daily lesson plans

❑ Formal and informal observations (relevant content)

 How am I going to do it?

❑ Formal and informal observations

❑ Remembering time and supplies needed

 How will I know they learned it?

❑ Portfolio of proof

❑ Assessment

 How will they use tomorrow what I am teaching them today?

Things to Consider

✓ Standardized Tests and Other Assessment Data

✓ Grade-Level Expectancies

✓ Performance Standards

✓ Instructional Guides

Troubleshooting a Lesson

Introduction

Time: _____

- ❖ What will the students be expected to do/know at the end?
- ❖ What is the purpose of the lesson?
- ❖ What motivational strategies are you planning to use?
- ❖ How does this lesson relate to previous learning?
- ❖ How does this lesson relate to other subject areas?
- ❖ What are your specific standards for the lesson?
- ❖ How will you communicate them to the children?

Instruction

Time: _____

- ❖ How/when are you planning to pass out materials?
- ❖ What materials do you expect the students to already have?
- ❖ How will the students be arranged in the classroom?
- ❖ Is your instruction detailed and in proper sequence?
- ❖ Is your modeling of the learning accurate and specific?

Guided Practice

Time: _____

- ❖ How are you going to check for understanding?
- ❖ Will the students participate in an activity?
- ❖ How will you know if they are experiencing success?
- ❖ What do the students do when they are finished?

Closure

Time: _____

- ❖ How will you end the guided practice?
- ❖ How will you re-focus their attention?
- ❖ Who will you re-state the objective?
- ❖ How will you evaluate the success of each individual student?
- ❖ How will you evaluate the success of the class?
- ❖ How will you evaluate your success as their teacher?

Independent Practice

- ❖ Will there be homework?
- ❖ Is the homework a practice of the new learning?

Graphic Organizers

Venn Diagram

The Venn diagram is made up of two or more overlapping circles. It is often used in mathematics to show relationships between sets. In language arts instruction, Venn diagrams are useful for examining similarities and differences in characters, stories, poems, etc.

A Venn diagram is frequently used as a prewriting activity to enable students to organize thoughts or textual quotations prior to writing a compare/contrast essay. This activity enables students to organize similarities and differences visually.

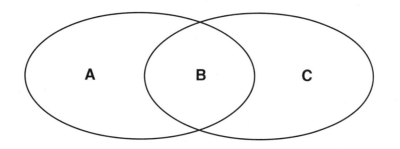

Fishbone Mapping

A fishbone map is used to show the causal interaction of a complex event (an election, a nuclear explosion, etc.) or complex phenomenon (juvenile delinquency, learning disabilities, etc.).

Key frame questions: What are the factors that cause X? How do they interrelate? Are the factors that cause X the same as those that cause X to persist?

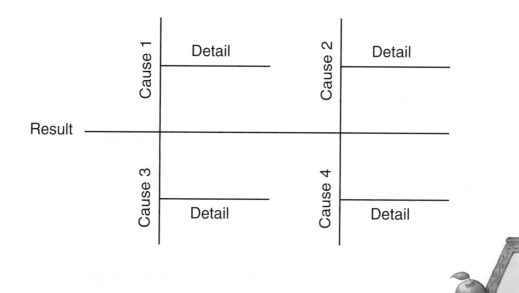

Graphic Organizers *(cont.)*

Spider Map

The spider map is used to describe a central idea—a thing, a process, a concept, or a proposition. The map may be used to organize ideas or brainstorm ideas for a writing project.

Key frame questions: What is the central idea? What are its attributes? What are its functions?

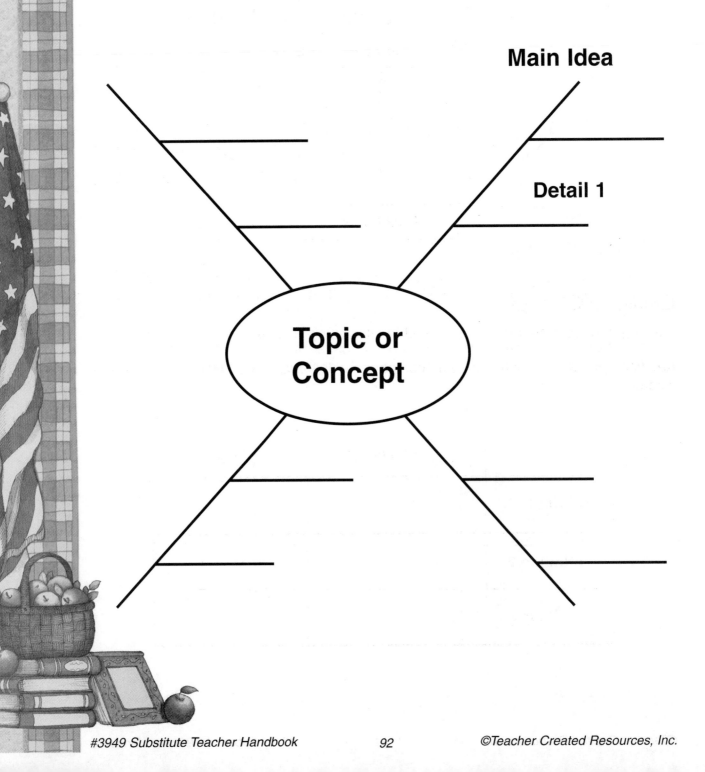

Main Idea

Detail 1

Topic or Concept

Graphic Organizers *(cont.)*

Chain of Events

Chain of events is an organizer used to describe the stages of an event, the actions of character, or the steps in a procedure.

Key questions: What is the first step in the procedure or initiating event? What are the next stages or steps? How does one event lead to one another? What is the final outcome?

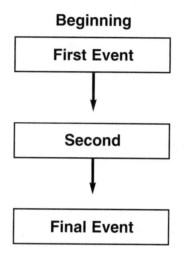

Compare/Contrast

The compare/contrast organizer is used to show similarities and differences.

Key frame questions: What is being compared? How are they similar? How are they different?

	Name 1	Name 2
Attribute 1		
Attribute 2		
Attribute 3		

Graphic Organizers *(cont.)*

Continuum

A continuum is used for time lines showing historical events, ages (e.g., grade levels in school), degrees of something (e.g., weight), shades of meaning, or rating scales (e.g., achievement in school).

Key frame questions: What is being scaled? What are the end points or extremes?

Low   High

Clustering

Clustering is a nonlinear activity that generates ideas, images, and feelings around a stimulus word. As students cluster, their thoughts tumble out, enlarging their word bank for writing and often enabling them to see patterns in their ideas. Clustering may be a class or individual activity.

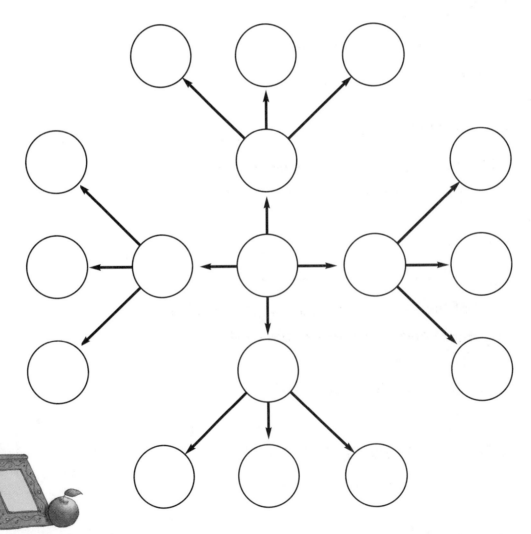

Lesson Plan Guide

Name:_____ Date: _____

Room:_____ Level: _____ Grade: _____

Subject: _____ Time: _____ # of Students: _____

Objective: _____

 ## Anticipatory Set

❑ Standards
❑ Transfer
❑ Purpose
❑ Motivation

 ## Instruction

❑ Direct teaching or discovery
❑ Check for understanding

 ## Guided Practice

❑ They practice what you just demonstrated.
❑ Teacher checks as they do their work.

 ## Closure

❑ Wrap up
❑ Help the students remember what they've learned.
❑ Lasting memory (whenever possible)

 ## Independent Practice

❑ Homework
❑ Independent project

100 Ways to Say "Good Job!"

We've noticed that teachers do not often vary their praise words. When "good" is used repeatedly, it loses its impact. Try these ways to say, "Good job!"

1. Good for you.
2. Wow!
3. That's great.
4. I like the way you did that.
5. Much better.
6. Keep it up.
7. It's a pleasure to see that.
8. What neat work.
9. This pleases me.
10. Terrific!
11. Beautiful!
12. Excellent work.
13. I appreciate your help.
14. Why don't you show the class?
15. Marvelous!
16. Fantastic!
17. Right on.
18. For sure.
19. Sharp!
20. That's going to be a great report.
21. How impressive.
22. You're on the right track.
23. That's "A" work.
24. It looks like you put a lot of work into this.
25. That's clever.
26. Very creative.
27. Good thinking.
28. Now you've got it.
29. Exactly right.
30. Super!
31. I couldn't have done it better myself.
32. Good point.
33. Good observation.
34. That's really nice.
35. You've got it now.
36. Nice going.
37. You made it look easy.
38. You've got it now.
39. That's good.
40. You're doing a good job.
41. That's it.
42. You're very good at that.
43. Now you've got it figured out.
44. I knew you could do it.
45. Keep working on it.
46. Now you have it.
47. You are learning fast.
48. One more time, and you'll have it.
49. That's the way to do it.
50. You did it that time!

100 Ways to Say "Good Job!" *(cont.)*

51. You're getting better and better.
52. You haven't missed a thing.
53. That's the way.
54. Well done.
55. Can't stop you now.
56. That's the way to do it.
57. Sensational!
58. Your brain is in gear today.
59. That's better.
60. This is first-class work.
61. Perfect!
62. Way to go.
63. Wonderful.
64. That's the best ever.
65. Exceptional work!
66. Super duper!
67. Cool!
68. You've been practicing.
69. You did that well.
70. Fine!
71. Outstanding.
72. Your're a pro!
73. Tremendous!
74. That's a fine job.
75. You're really improving.

76. Superb!
77. Good remembering!
78. You've got it down pat.
79. You sure did well.
80. Right again!
81. I like that.
82. I'm impressed!
83. You're unstoppable!
84. Very interesting.
85. You've got the hang of it.
86. Keep on trying!
87. Very good job.
88. You remembered.
89. That's really nice.
90. Thanks!
91. What neat work.
92. Superior work.
93. Nicely done.
94. You make it look easy.
95 It's coming along nicely.
96. You aced it!
97. I'm proud of you.
98. You make me proud.
99. Out of sight!
100. It's one of your best.

Chapter 5

Emergency Curriculum

Sponge Activities

Overview

Sponge activities are quick activities that are designed to teach something in a short period of time. However, they are not time wasters! The following pages include sponge activities for primary-grade students (pages 100 and 101), intermediate-grade students (pages 102 and 103), and high school students (page 104 and 105).

The sponges listed in this section are flexible in the following ways:

✓ most can be adjusted to different grade levels

✓ many can be either oral or written

✓ many can be used as beginning sponges, transition sponges, or dismissal sponges.

Use the sponge prompts on pages 100–105 to trigger other ideas of your own.

Tips for Using Sponge Activities

❖ Mark the sponge activities that look especially good to you so that you can find them easily.

❖ Sponge activities should be about five minutes long. If you need to fill up more time, consider combining two sponges.

Sponge Activities

For Primary-Grade Students

1. Have students clap out the syllables in their names, spelling words, fruits, vegetables, etc.

2. State numbers, days of the week, or months of the year in order and pause. Then call on students to tell what comes next.

3. State two numbers; call on a student to state the missing number.

4. State one number; call on a student to state the numbers that come before and after that number.

5. Write a word on the board; students either state or write words that rhyme.

6. Count as a class to 100; do this by 2's, 5's, 10's, etc.

7. Play "Hangman" using categories such as animals, meat, flowers, etc.

8. Play "Simon Says."

9. Play "I Spy" by stating items in the room that either begin with a certain letter, are a certain color, are made of plastic, are in a certain shape, etc.

10. Find little words within a big word.

11. Say a word that has a short vowel sound or begins with a particular consonant blend; call on a student to say a like word.

12. Play "I Am Going on a Trip." State an item to take along that begins with "A"; students add to list one by one in alphabetical order.

13. Have students add up the numbers in a series of phone numbers.

Sponge Activities

For Primary-Grade Students *(cont.)*

14. Count backwards together from 50 to 1.

15. Have students scramble five of their spelling words, trade papers, and unscramble the words.

16. Have students state one playground rule, one good health habit, one safety rule, etc., as they are dismissed.

17. State a word; call on a student to state its opposite.

18. Using small numbers, state an ongoing math problem (e.g., 1 + 2 + 3 + 4). Students try to keep up with their answers.

19. Have students list the alphabet down the left side of their paper. Allow five minutes for students to try to write a word that begins with each letter of the alphabet.

20. Display spelling words with blanks (for example, l _ _ k). Students complete as many words as they can within a time limit.

21. Write a compound word on the board. Children use the last word of the compound word as the first word of a new compound. This continues, with the goal being to make the longest possible chain of compound words.

22. Give three or more oral directions, such as "Hop three times. Touch your left foot. Turn around twice." Students must follow the directions.

23. Write words on the board. Call out a word. Have a student find the word, use it in a sentence, and erase it. Then dismiss him or her.

24. Think of a vocabulary word, book title, color, etc. Students try to identify the word by playing "Twenty Questions," asking only questions that can be answered by "yes" or "no."

25. Write a letter on the chalkboard. Students have two minutes to write as many words as they can that begin with that letter.

Sponge Activities

For Intermediate-Grade Students

1. State or write a number sequence. Students figure out the pattern and tell what number comes next.

2. Count to 100 by 3's, 7's, etc. You can have students do this together; or they can do this individually, and you can check their progress by circulating around the room.

3. Play "Hangman." Use new and difficult vocabulary words.

4. Write a long word on the board. Students get two minutes to see how many smaller words they can make using the letters from the long word.

5. Play "I Am Going on a Trip." Teacher states an item to take along that begins with "A"; students must repeat previous items, and then add to the list in alphabetical order.

6. Write scrambled words on the board (spelling words, vocabulary words, science terms, countries, etc.). Students unscramble as many words as they can within a specified time limit.

7. State or write a word. Call on a student to tell a synonym, an antonym, or a homonym.

8. State verbal ongoing math problem, such as "Start with 6, square it, subtract 1, divide by 7, multiply by 9." Students try to keep up with the problem and end with the correct answer.

9. List 5–10 words on the board. Have students put them in alphabetical order within one minute.

10. Have students write the alphabet down the left side of the paper. Within a specified time limit, students write a word that begins with as many letters as possible. Categories can be animals, foods, trees, adjectives, etc.

11. Write words on board with beginning and ending letters only (e.g., b_ _ _ _ t). Have students think of words that fit the pattern. Words should have at least five letters.

12. Allow three to five minutes for students to make a list of words related to a given category, such as "circus."

Sponge Activities

For Intermediate-Grade Students *(cont.)*

13. Play "Twenty Questions" with famous people, TV programs, sports, cities, etc. Students ask questions that can only be answered with "yes" or "no."

14. Have students draw something made only of circles (or triangles, rectangles, etc.).

15. Write words, phrases, or titles on the board without the vowels (e.g., "tch," "Chrltt's Wb," "Tdy's Flg Dy"). Students try to identify the missing letters.

16. Have students print their names vertically along the left margins of their papers. Then have them write an adjective to describe themselves beginning with each of the letters.

17. Think of a word. Give students a rhyming word clue (e.g., "My word rhymes with *set*"). The class guesses by asking questions, such as "Is your word a fast airplane?"

18. Write scrambled sentences on the board (e.g., "chocolate like ice I cream"). Students unscramble as many sentences as they can within a specified time limit.

19. State a category such as "fruit" and a number over five. Students list words whose combined number of syllables total the given number (e.g., banana + apple + cantaloupe + orange + grape = 10)

20. Write a four-letter word on a board (e.g., "card"). Students form a new word by changing one letter (e.g., care, cord, cart, hard). Words are arranged like a ladder. The goal is to see how long they can make the ladder.

21. List words on board. Students use words to make a "word design" that is similar to a crossword puzzle.

22. Name all the continents of the world.

23. Make up three names for rock groups.

24. How many countries and their capitals can you name?

25. How many baseball teams can you name?

26. Tell students to turn to their neighbors. One of them will tell the other about an interesting experience they have had. The listener must be prepared to re-tell the story to the class.

27. List five parts of the body above the neck that have three letters.

Sponge Activities

For High School Students

1. Come up with as many inventions as you can think of that could be foot-operated.

2. Come up with as many homonyms (words that sound alike but look different) as you can.

3. Sketch an idea for an art project you can eat.

4. Work with a partner to come up with 20 ideas for using a cement block.

5. What's the longest word you know? Write it on a piece of paper, and then come up with as many words as you can think of that are made from those letters.

6. Predict the most popular months for birthdays, and then chart those in your class. Do the same for birthday dates.

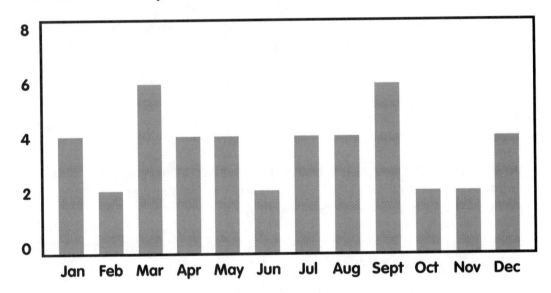

7. Think of 10 ways to get rid of unwanted paper.

8. Give students examples of square roots. If they don't know the term already, then have them estimate the square root of some large numbers, like 540, 27,000, or 8,000,000.

9. Have students describe the first place they would take a foreign visitor to and explain why that place is important to them.

10. Discuss mascots or symbols that would be more appropriate for political parties.

11. Have students come up with two or three new political parties and what they would stand for.

Sponge Activities

For High School Students *(cont.)*

12. What if buildings were made of flexible materials? What are some advantages and disadvantages? What would it be like to be in one? What affect would weather have?

13. Have students make their own "business cards" (use the school's address and phone for privacy, if you like), using their own paper, pens, and markers. They can even include a "business" of their own creation. Then staple them all to a bulletin board. Working within a five-minute parameter gives them a tight, real-world "deadline" to focus on.

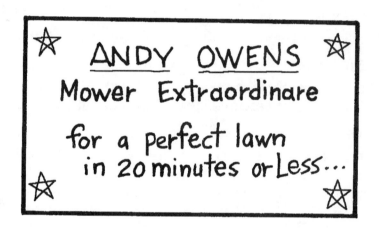

14. Ask a student to describe a Global Positioning System device. Brainstorm interesting uses for one.

15. Have students brainstorm how the world seems to be designed for older adults and explain what they would like to see to make them feel more comfortable or important.

16. Have students discuss what they would do if they were the president of the United States in this political climate.

17. Have students list as many U.S. presidents as they can.

18. Have students list as many country capitals as they can.

19. Ask students how many parts of an automobile they can list.

20. Have students list 25 breakfast cereals that they would find in a grocery store.

21. Ask students to name the president, vice president, secretary of state, and one other cabinet member of the United States.

22. Have students list all the musical instruments that begin with the letter "T."

Language Arts Lessons

Pages 106–109 contain easy, adaptable language arts lessons. The ideas on these pages are designed to help you fill any unplanned time with meaningful activities. Keep that in mind when you choose something to do. Mix and match all of these suggested assignments. If you see something you like from a different grade level, make it fit your class.

Subject: Pets

Theme: Make an imaginary pet out of scraps. Name your pet.

❖ *For 1st or 2nd graders*

Write two to three sentences about your pet. Share with the class.

❖ *For 3rd graders*

Write a descriptive paragraph about your pet and share with the class.

❖ *For 4th or 5th graders*

Write two to three paragraphs about your animal. Make sure each paragraph talks about a separate idea. Share with the class.

❖ *For 6th graders*

Adopt an imaginary pet and write a letter to your parents explaining why you should be able to have this animal. Outline the care the animal would have to have daily, weekly, and annually. Share with the class.

Subject: Pets

Theme: Staple several sheets of paper together to make a book about your pet.

❖ *For 1st or 2nd graders*

On each page give one or two facts about your animal. Illustrate and share with the class.

❖ *For 3rd graders*

Write a narrative story telling what happened when your pet got loose in a museum. Illustrate it and share with the class.

❖ *For 4th graders*

Use the book to design a house for your pet by showing all the steps and describing how it is made. Share with another student to see if he or she understands your directions.

❖ *For 5th or 6th graders*

Write your own fairy tale using animals as the characters. Change the plot around so that the protagonist and the antagonist change places. Illustrate your story and share with the class.

Language Arts Lessons *(cont.)*

Subject: Electricity

Background: Benjamin Franklin invented the lightning rod that protected people from the power of electricity inside lightning.

Theme: Electricity does many things for people. If there were no electricity, how would we be affected?

❖ *For 1st graders*

Find items in the room that are run by electricity. Draw them and tell what you would do without them.

❖ *For 2nd graders*

Choose three things from home that run on electricity. Draw them and tell what you would do without them.

❖ *For 3rd graders*

Pick an appliance and invent a machine that would do the same task without electricity. Tell how it would be the same as and different than what we currently use.

❖ *For 4th graders*

Tell how the United States would have developed without the aid of electricity. Would we live the same as our ancestors, or would we have developed a completely different society?

❖ *For 5th or 6th graders*

Invent a new source of energy and explain how we would use it to power machines. Illustrate your concept.

Subject: Electricity

Theme: Things at home and school use electricity.

❖ *For 1st graders*

List and illustrate items in the classroom that run on electricity.

❖ *For 2nd graders:*

Write a sentence about four different things that run on electricity and tell how they have helped you in the past week.

❖ *For 3rd graders*

Write a paragraph about the dangers of sticking one's finger in a light socket. Be sure to include all the parts of a paragraph (opening, detail sentences, and closing sentence). Illustrate.

❖ *For 4th or 5th graders*

Write a narrative about yourself going back 100 years to sell electric appliances. How would you convince our ancestors to buy your new products?

❖ *For 6th graders*

Write and present a TV commercial selling a completely new electric device.

Language Arts Lessons *(cont.)*

Subject: Telephones

Background: Alexander Graham Bell became famous when he invented the telephone.

Theme: Phones are constantly changing.

❖ *For 1st or 2nd graders*

Draw a picture of yourself using a phone in the future. Explain how you would use it.

❖ *For 3rd or 4th graders*

Phones are getting smaller. Design a phone that can fit in your ear. Write a paragraph about how you would use it, speak into it, or dial a number. Illustrate a magazine advertisement for this.

❖ *For 5th graders*

Discuss the evolution of phones. Write a three-paragraph essay on different styles of phones and the service they require.

❖ *For 6th graders*

Become Alexander Graham Bell and defend your position that the telephone in its original form was a better device than what we have today. Present your ideas to the class and defend your position.

Theme: Design your own phone.

❖ *For 1st or 2nd graders*

Use construction paper to create your new design for a new phone. Write two to three sentences about it.

❖ *For 3rd graders*

Most phones are getting smaller. Create one that is a larger version and must hang from the ceiling. Write a paragraph telling why this is a good idea.

❖ *For 4th graders*

Create a three-dimensional model of a phone. Write a paragraph explaining how to use your telephone.

❖ *For 5th or 6th graders*

Create a three-dimensional telephone, complete with three-dimensional buttons and an ear piece. Write a letter to a friend bragging about the new phone you just bought for $1,000. Explain why it's such a good choice for you.

Language Arts Lessons *(cont.)*

Subject: Automobiles

Background: Henry Ford didn't invent the automobile. Instead, he found a way of making them much cheaper by using an assembly line. By doing this, he created a way in which more people could afford to own one.

Theme: Vehicles and their motors

❖ *For 1st graders*

Draw a picture of a car that has no motor. Write two sentences telling how it works.

❖ *For 2nd graders*

Draw a picture of a car and tell of all the things you can think of that are needed for the car to run.

❖ *For 3rd or 4th graders*

Draw a picture of the first car you can remember that your family owned. Compare it to the car you have now. Why was it a good decision to buy the car you have now?

❖ *For 5th or 6th graders*

Henry Ford became famous for using the assembly line. Write several paragraphs telling what you know about this process. Tell what robots may now do to build cars as opposed to the past where people had to handle each part. Explain why either the new or the old system of assembly was better.

Extension Idea: How about adding a survey with one of these assignments? The students can find out which cars their families drive and make a chart. Younger children can investigate the colors of their parents' cars.

Language Arts Games

Pages 110 and 111 contain quick and fun language arts games.

Word Bowl

1. Gather 10 plastic bottles, each partially filled with sand. These will be used for bowling pins.

2. Write spelling words on ten 3" x 5" index cards, one word per card. Going from 1 to 10, put one number on the back of each card.

3. Attach the words to the bottles with masking tape with the number side in view.

4. Use a rubber ball as a bowling ball.

5. The student rolls the ball at the pins.

6. His or her partner stands by the pins and reads the words on the bottles that have been knocked down.

7. If the bowler can spell the words, the numbers on the cards are totaled for his or her score.

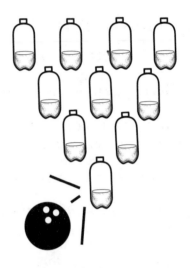

Antonym Toss

1. Use a piece of yarn stretched across the room.

2. Divide the class into two teams.

3. One child on the first team tosses an eraser or beanbag over the net.

4. The child who catches the eraser or beanbag must call out a word with an opposite meaning.

5. That child throws it back across, and the opposing person who catches it must say the antonym.

6. If the answer is correct, the answering team gets a point.

7. The second child calls out a word, tosses the object across the net, and the procedure is repeated.

Language Arts Games (cont.)

Word Bounce

1. Write simple sentences on cards. Divide class into small groups.

2. Each group selects a card and stands in a line.

3. The first child says the first word in the sentence, bounces the ball the same number of times as the number of syllables in the sentence, and passes the ball.

4. The game continues in this manner until all the cards have been used.

Pigeon Hole Toss

1. Use a cardboard box with packing sections or filing trays.

2. Place a color tab on each section (e.g., orange, blue, red, yellow).

3. Prepare a set of word cards and color-code the word cards to correspond with the colors used on the packing box.

4. The student tosses a beanbag at the box.

5. If the beanbag lands in the red section, the teacher takes a word card with that color and pronounces the word.

6. The student spells the word and uses it in a sentence.

7. If the student spells the word correctly and uses it correctly in a sentence, he or she receives two points.

Password

1. Place students in two to three teams.

2. Give one person on each team a vocabulary word.

3. That person gives their team a one-word clue, and the team tries to guess the word.

4. Go to the next team for the same procedure.

5. Continue the process until one team guesses the word.

Chalkboard Topics
For Those Who Finish Early

In your bag of tricks, include a list of assignments that you can quickly put up on the chalkboard. Often, you can keep the students out of trouble if you can keep them busy. Either write some of these on the board, make a portable poster of them, or run copies off for everyone. That way when students are done with their work, you can simply refer them to a specific assignment number.

Assignment Examples

1. Find the meanings of these words: *emulate, arrogant, ascetic, tolerant,* and *dogmatic.* Use each in a sentence.
2. Locate the titles and names of the persons in the president's cabinet.
3. Find the names of the heads of state in the following countries: Britain, France, Russia, and Germany.
4. In one paragraph, give information about a famous person. Choose from the following people: Tiger Woods, Toni Morrison, George W. Bush, or Albert Einstein.
5. About what percentage of the Earth's surface is covered by water?
6. Which of these animals will generally live the longest: mosquito, barn owl, alligator, or zebra?
7. Is coral an animal, a plant, or neither?
8. How long a line can an average 7-inch pencil draw (1-inch stub remaining)?
9. Which kills more people in the United States each year, bullets from handguns or traffic crashes?
10. Can your bones be considered part of your circulatory system?
11. What does the appendix do?
12. What is your body's largest organ? What is its second largest?
13. How many bones are in your body?
14. What is the largest African country in terms of area?
15. Which European country (excluding Russia) has the largest population?
16. Which Asian country has the largest population?
17. Where is the tallest mountain in the world?

Last-Minute English Lessons

❖ In-Class Essay

Writing Situation: If you've lived in a family for any length of time, you can't help hearing a story or two about some member of the family. The main character of the story might be an aunt, uncle, or grandparent. The story may have taken place during a special holiday or special family outing. This story could be entertaining or might teach a lesson.

Directions for Writing: Write a story about your family for a literary magazine. This story should be one you have heard repeated during family gatherings. It might be amusing, or it might instill family pride. The characters, setting, and event should be well defined and real. This story might even include a moral. Make sure to tell the reader why this story is important to your family.

❖ Dictionary Relay

Give each row/team of students a list of words and a dictionary. The first student in each row is to look up the top word on the list, write down the guide words (the two words at the top of a dictionary page; they show the first and last entries on the page) from the page on which it appears and passes the list and the dictionary to the next student. The first row/team to complete the list wins.

Guide Words

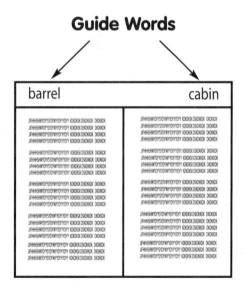

❖ Literature Response for Characterization

Think about some of the characters you have read about this year. Brainstorm for names and the novels or stories with which they are connected. In a one-page response, describe a favorite character and tell why he or she was memorable to you.

Last-Minute English Lessons *(cont.)*

❖ In-Class Essay

Ask students to write one paragraph stating three promises they would make to voters if they were running for president of the United States. Have students take turns sharing one or more of the promises.

❖ Time Line

Have students draw a time line on a poster, beginning with the date they were born and extending to the present year. On parallel lines, students should list important historical events and important personal events. Have a class discussion about times when important historical events intersect with important events in students' lives.

❖ Be a Historian

As a class, brainstorm historical figures that stand out in your mind. Answer "who, what, when, where, and why" for each person. Have students write a one-paragraph mini-biography of that person and share it with the class.

❖ Recreating a Great American Speech

Writing Situation: Create a transparency of the Gettysburg Address (page 115) and use it so that students may reference it during their writing assignment. This famous speech was given by President Lincoln in November of 1863 to commemorate and honor the thousands of soldiers who died at the Battle of Gettysburg in July of 1863. What did President Lincoln say about the Civil War and the nation?

Directions for Writing: Read the Gettysburg Address (page 115) and rewrite it in your own words. If you are not certain what a word means, look up its meaning in a dictionary.

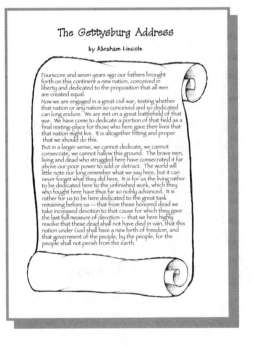

The Gettysburg Address

by Abraham Lincoln

Fourscore and seven years ago our fathers brought forth on this continent a new nation, conceived in liberty and dedicated to the proposition that all men are created equal.

Now we are engaged in a great civil war, testing whether that nation or any nation so conceived and so dedicated can long endure. We are met on a great battlefield of that war. We have come to dedicate a portion of that field as a final resting-place for those who here gave their lives that that nation might live. It is altogether fitting and proper that we should do this.

But in a larger sense, we cannot dedicate, we cannot consecrate, we cannot hallow this ground. The brave men, living and dead who struggled here have consecrated it far above our poor power to add or detract. The world will little note nor long remember what we say here, but it can never forget what they did here. It is for us the living rather to be dedicated here to the unfinished work, which they who fought here have thus far so nobly advanced. It is rather for us to be here dedicated to the great task remaining before us -- that from these honored dead we take increased devotion to that cause for which they gave the last full measure of devotion -- that we here highly resolve that these dead shall not have died in vain, that this nation under God shall have a new birth of freedom, and that government of the people, by the people, for the people shall not perish from the earth.

The Gettysburg Address

by Abraham Lincoln

Fourscore and seven years ago our fathers brought forth on this continent a new nation, conceived in liberty and dedicated to the proposition that all men are created equal.

Now we are engaged in a great civil war, testing whether that nation or any nation so conceived and so dedicated can long endure. We are met on a great battlefield of that war. We have come to dedicate a portion of that field as a final resting-place for those who here gave their lives that that nation might live. It is altogether fitting and proper that we should do this.

But in a larger sense, we cannot dedicate, we cannot consecrate, we cannot hallow this ground. The brave men, living and dead who struggled here have consecrated it far above our poor power to add or detract. The world will little note nor long remember what we say here, but it can never forget what they did here. It is for us the living rather to be dedicated here to the unfinished work, which they who fought here have thus far so nobly advanced. It is rather for us to be here dedicated to the great task remaining before us -- that from these honored dead we take increased devotion to that cause for which they gave the last full measure of devotion -- that we here highly resolve that these dead shall not have died in vain, that this nation under God shall have a new birth of freedom, and that government of the people, by the people, for the people shall not perish from the earth.

Practice Test 1
Punctuation, Capitalization, & Grammar

Name: _____

Directions: Each of the following sentences contains at least two errors. Correct them and rewrite them on the lines provided.

1. dr. tripp is my english teacher.

   _____

2. The university of aizu is a new university in japan.

   _____

3. Los angeles is the most populated city in california

   _____

4. She wrote a book called <u>the healthy persons guide to eating</u>

   _____

5. i read a chapter called physical maps of africa

   _____

6. my too favorite sports is football and soccer.

   _____

7. The poor puppy hurt it's paw

   _____

8. Sam had four shiney pennys in his pocket.

   _____

9. His uncle Jack fought in world war II.

   _____

10. Educational technology news is my favorite magazine.

    _____

11. The japanese and the english both live on islands off the coasts of major continents.

    _____

12. Did both lawyer's leave there briefcases in the courtroom.

    _____

Practice Test II
Punctuation, Capitalization, & Grammar

Name: _____

Directions: Correct any punctuation, capitalization, or grammar errors in the following sentences. Rewrite them on the lines provided.

1. The gooses migrated back to oregon recently.

   _____

2. It might rain today and Steve and I forgot to bring our umbrellas.

   _____

3. senator moore said, I will work hard to be a good senator.

   _____

4. "How," I asked "Can you always be so forgetful"?

   _____

5. The declaration of independence was signed on july 4 1776 in philadelphia pennsylvania.

   _____

6. Where did Mrs Roberts go to school Yale or Harvard.

   _____

7. Who's car is parked in your neighbors driveway?

   _____

8. My mother in law will arrive on the 456 P.M. train.

   _____

9. As a result of his embezzling the company went bankrupt.

   _____

10. I learned to play row, row, row your boat on the trumpet.

    _____

11. Tara enjoys reading writing and listening to music but she doesn't like to play sports.

    _____

12. Both boys bicycles are broken so they have to walk to school.

    _____

Practice Test III
Punctuation, Capitalization, & Grammar

Name: _____

Directions: Read the paragraph in the box. Rewrite it on the lines below. Correct any punctuation, capitalization, or grammar errors.

Have you ever had a chocolate chip cookie. Americans eat 7 billion of them each year. Few know that these cookies were invented accidently in 1930. Ruth Wakefield ran the toll house inn in Massachusetts. She make food for the guests. One day as she mixed up a batch of chocolate cookies she realized that she was out of bakers chocolate. She broke a chocolate bar into tiney peaces. She add the chocolate bits to the dough hoping they would melt and spread throughout the cookies. When she took the cookie sheets from the oven, ruth was upset to sea that the chocolate chunks were still their. However, a guest wanted to try a cookie. He couldnt believe how good it tasted. Other guests ate the cookies and liked them too. Ruth wakefield had just invented chocolate chip cookies.

_____

_____

_____

_____

_____

_____

_____

_____

_____

_____

_____

Practice Tests

Answer Key

Practice Test I

1. Dr. Tripp is my English teacher.
2. The University of Aizu is a new university in Japan.
3. Los Angeles is the most populated city in California.
4. She wrote a book called <u>The Healthy Person's Guide to Eating</u>.
5. I read a chapter called "Physical Maps of Africa."
6. My two favorite sports are football and soccer.
7. The poor puppy hurt its paw.
8. Sam had four shiny pennies in his pocket.
9. His Uncle Jack fought in World War II.
10. <u>Educational Technology News</u> is my favorite magazine.
11. The Japanese and the English both live on islands off the coasts of major continents.
12. Did both lawyers leave their briefcases in the courtroom?

Practice Test II

1. The geese migrated back to Oregon recently.
2. It might rain today, and Steve and I forgot to bring our umbrellas.
3. Senator Moore said, "I will work hard to be a good senator."
4. "How," I asked, "can you always be so forgetful?"
5. The Declaration of Independence was signed on July 4, 1776, in Philadelphia, Pennsylvania.
6. Where did Mrs. Roberts go to school, Yale or Harvard?
7. Whose car is parked in your neighbor's driveway?
8. My mother-in-law will arrive on the 4:56 P.M. train.
9. As a result of his embezzling, the company went bankrupt.
10. I learned to play "Row, Row, Row Your Boat" on the trumpet.
11. Tara enjoys reading, writing, and listening to music, but she doesn't like to play sports.
12. Both boys' bicycles are broken, so they have to walk to school.

Practice Test III

Have you ever had a chocolate chip cookie? Americans eat 7 billion of them each year. Few know that these cookies were invented accidentally in 1930. Ruth Wakefield ran the Toll House Inn in Massachusetts. She made food for the guests. One day as she mixed up a batch of chocolate cookies, she realized that she was out of baker's chocolate. She broke a chocolate bar into tiny pieces. She added the chocolate bits to the dough, hoping they would melt and spread throughout the cookies. When she took the cookie sheets from the oven, Ruth was upset to see that the chocolate chunks were still there. However, a guest wanted to try a cookie. He couldn't believe how good it tasted. Other guests ate the cookies and liked them, too. Ruth Wakefield had just invented chocolate chip cookies.

Note: Use the word search on page 120 to test student's knowledge of homophones. (See the answers to the right.) Fill in the blank word search puzzle on page 121 with words from a story or unit of study. Make copies and have students solve the word search puzzle that you have created.

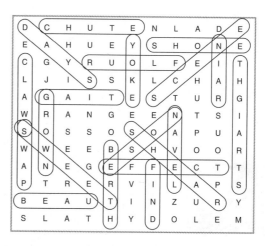

Homophones Word Search

Directions: Homophones are words that have the same sound but have different meaning. In the puzzle below, find the homophones for the following words:

fined	suite	bow
seen	reign, rein	shown
affect	shoot	yolk
flower	pause	sheer
birth	clause	gate
daze	knows	strait
naval	groan	

D	C	H	U	T	E	N	L	A	D	E
E	A	H	U	E	Y	S	H	O	N	E
C	G	Y	R	U	O	L	F	E	I	T
L	J	I	S	S	K	L	C	H	A	H
A	G	A	I	T	E	S	T	U	R	G
W	R	A	N	G	E	E	N	T	S	I
S	O	S	S	O	S	O	A	P	U	A
W	W	E	E	B	S	H	V	O	O	R
A	N	E	G	E	F	F	E	C	T	T
P	T	R	E	R	V	I	L	A	P	S
B	E	A	U	T	I	N	Z	U	R	Y
S	L	A	T	H	Y	D	O	L	E	M

Story Word Search

Directions: Hidden in the word search below are words from our story. Find as many as you can.

Fill-in-the-Blanks Lesson

"Build A New Story"

Grade Level: 3–6

Time: 30 minutes

Objective: Students will recreate old nursery rhymes with new parts of speech.

Materials: paper and pencil

Directions: Each student will work with a partner. Student asks their partners to fill in the necessary parts of speech. They read the story only after it is finished. Once they've finished with this one, they are to write down a nursery rhyme of their own, take out the same parts of speech, and start the process once again.

Hey diddle diddle,

The _____ and the _____ .
        (noun)   (noun)

The cow _____ _____ the _____ .
       (verb)   (preposition)   (noun)

The little dog _____ to see such _____
           (verb)   (noun)

And the dish _____ away with the _____ .
        (verb)   (noun)

The original goes like this:

"The Cat and the Fiddle"

Hey diddle diddle,

The cat and the fiddle,

The cow jumped over the moon.

The little dog laughed to see such sport,

And the dish ran away with the spoon.

Creative Writing Lesson

"Clouds"

Grade Level: primary grades

Time: 35–40 minutes

Objective: Develop writing skills while describing and developing a cloud shape.

Materials: large white construction paper and large colored construction paper

Directions: Begin by asking students if they have ever looked at clouds and discovered shapes in them (for instance, a bear, rabbit, etc.). Show students some shapes that have been torn from white construction paper. Ask them what they see in this shape. Does it look like a turtle, an ice-cream cone, etc.?

Explain to students that they are going to tear the large white construction paper into cloud shapes. No scissors allowed. Have the students return to their desks and tear the paper. Then have them turn in torn cloud shapes. Mix up all the torn shapes. Tell students they will receive someone else's shape. They will then glue it on the large colored construction paper and color it to resemble whatever animal or object they can see in its shape. Tell students when they have finished creating their picture, they are to write about it on the lined paper and glue it on the back.

At this point, review rules of writing by asking such questions as, "What does a sentence start with?" "What does a sentence end with?" "What is a sentence?" and "How can you make your sentence more interesting?" As students are working, give individual help with spelling and writing. Finish by gathering together and sharing work.

Creative Writing Lesson

"Collect a Story"

Grade Level: 3–6

Time: 45 minutes

Objective: Students will build stories, with everyone working together on every story.

Materials: paper and pencil

Directions: Everyone comes up with an idea for a story (for example, "A man wakes up to find his family has disappeared," "A nuclear accident causes it to rain vegetables," or "Pigs start walking on two legs and talking."). Let your students come up with imaginative ideas for story starters, and have the class vote on their favorite.

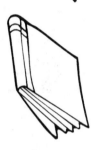

Once the idea is written on every student's paper, each student passes his or her paper to the next person. That person will add a few sentences (no more than four) before he or she passes it on to the next person. This continues until everyone has had a chance to build on every story.

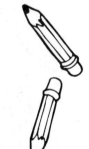

Everyone gets to read his or her story to the class. The class then decides which stories show good plot, character, and problem/solution development.

Creative Writing Lesson

"Collect a Sentence"

Grade Level: 3–6

Time: 15 minutes

Objective: Students will use the names of objects around them to create sentences.

Materials: paper and pencil

Directions: Give your students a time limit of approximately five minutes, and let them use that time to "collect" words they see out their windows or around the room. These can include the names of objects, descriptions of the items they see and hear (such as "blue" for the sky, "tall" for skyscrapers, "rumbling" for motors, and so on) and actual words your students find from signs. Have them write down as many of these words as they can in the time given. When you say "Time's up," they switch lists and use the words their neighbor collected to create as many sentences—serious or zany—as they can.

Students can work independently, in pairs, or as a team to create as many sentences as possible. After they have done this several times, their goal might be to beat their own "personal best" number of sentences from the previous round.

Poetry Lesson

"Cinquain"

Grade Level: 2–6

Time: one class period

Objective: Students will create a poem that includes descriptive words and action words.

Materials: paper and pencil

Directions: Discuss different types of poetry. Share some of your favorites and ask the students to share any they know. Next, tell the students that they are going to create a poem that shows action and describing words. It is called a cinquain. Make a sample on the board showing this pattern:

_____
one-word subject

_____ _____ _____
two or three descriptive words about the subject

_____ _____ _____
three action words describing the subject

_____
a short sentence or phrase describing how the subject makes you feel

_____
repeat of line 1 (or a synonym of that word)

Poetry Lesson

"Acrostic"

Grade Level: 2–6

Time: 15–30 minutes

Objective: Students will build a poem showing their own personality traits.

Materials: paper and pencil

Directions: Explain to the students that they are going to write a poem all about themselves. Have each student write his or her name vertically in capital letters. After each letter, students write a word that describes them and begins with that letter. Demonstrate an acrostic poem on the board.

Here is an example:

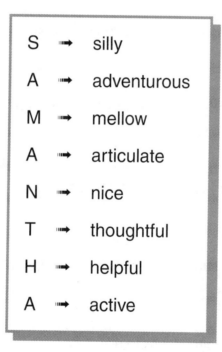

S ➡ silly

A ➡ adventurous

M ➡ mellow

A ➡ articulate

N ➡ nice

T ➡ thoughtful

H ➡ helpful

A ➡ active

Poetry Lesson

"Diamante"

Grade Level: 5–6

Time: one class period

Objective: Students will use different parts of speech to build a poem.

Materials: paper and pencil

Directions: A diamante is an unrhymed poem written in the shape of a diamond. The verse contains contrasting subjects and their describing words and verbs.

1. _____
   one (1) noun (indicating the subject or title)

2. _____ _____
   two (2) adjectives (describing the subject in line one)

3. _____ _____ _____
   three (3) -ing or -ed words (which relate to the subject in line 1)

4. _____ _____ _____ _____
   four (4) nouns (which relate to the subject in line 1)

5. _____ _____ _____
   three (3) -ing or -ed words (which relate to the subject in line 7)

6. _____ _____
   two (2) adjectives (describing the subject in line 7)

7. _____
   one (1) noun (the opposite of the subject in line 1)

Last-Minute Math Lessons

❖ Quick Move

1. Write numbers from 1–10 on 3" x 5" index cards (two sets).

2. Make up two teams, each with four to five players.

3. Each child receives two cards.

4. The teacher calls out a number (e.g., 17).

5. The team members answer the problem by hopping up to the front of the room with the correct combination of cards (e.g., 7 and 10; 8 and 9; etc.).

❖ Rebound

1. Write arithmetic problems on large pieces of construction paper or cardboard. Allow four inches of the paper to bend, and attach each card to the floor with masking tape. Place cards 12 inches apart.

2. The cards are standing up and placed in front of a wall.

3. The first child gently rolls a ball toward the wall, and it should rebound off the wall and roll over a number.

4. If the child answers the problem correctly, attach a new card over that number with a paper clip.

5. The child receives one point for each correct answer.

❖ Number Bounce

1. The children are numbered and stand in a circle, with one child in the center.

2. That child is given a number (e.g., 8) by the teacher.

3. To start the game, the teacher holds up a stimulus card showing a process sign (e.g., x).

4. The child in the center bounces a ball to another child and says his number (e.g., 8).

5. The one who catches the ball gives his own number (e.g., 5) and combines the two in a multiplication problem (i.e., 8 x 5 = 40).

6. If the answer is incorrect, then he or she takes a turn in the center of the circle. The teacher calls out another number and holds up another process sign, and the game continues in the above manner.

Last-Minute Math Lessons *(cont.)*

❖ Relay Math

1. Students are numbered off into groups of three.

2. Each group gets a handout sheet with 20 various math problems.

3. Person "A" has 1½ minutes to independently work on as many problems as he or she can. Next, person "B" does the same thing. Finally, Person "C" works for the same amount of time. Each member may choose to do a new problem or redo one that is already completed.

4. Team members who aren't working must not give any help.

5. Next, the team members will each have one minute to work uninterrupted.

6. Finally, each member gets 30 seconds to finish or correct anything they choose.

7. The team with the most correct answers wins.

❖ Battleship

1. Give all students a piece of graph paper.

2. Students pair up and draw identical (6 x 6) grids as their partner.

3. Each student should label the squares of the grid with numbers going down the side and letters going across the top. (See the sample grid below.)

3. Each person in the pair colors in 10 squares on their grid.

4. Without looking, they take turns trying to find the squares on their opponent's grid.

5. The first person to find all their opponent's squares is the winner.

Sample Battleship Grid

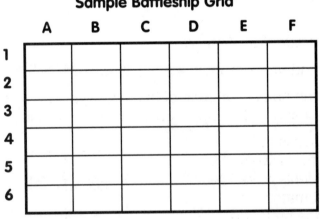

❖ Multiplication War

1. Children use only the numbered cards in a deck of cards.

2. They turn over cards as they would if they were playing a game of war.

3. They must multiply the numbers on the two cards.

4. The player with the first correct answer gets both cards.

5. Play until one person has all the cards.

6. You may want to assign a number value to aces and face cards (i.e., kings, queens, and jacks) if you wish to use them.

Last-Minute Math Lessons (cont.)

❖ Baseball

1. Divide your class into two teams, and then tell the class where the batter will stand.

2. Determine where the bases will be.

3. Give the batter a question or math fact to answer.

4. If he or she gets it right, he or she moves to 1st base. If the student misses it, that is an out.

5. Students chalk up their runs on the board as they come in. The other team sits in their seats and holds up fingers to show the number of outs.

❖ Heads Up, 7 Up (With a New Twist)

1. You pick seven children who come up front while the others put their heads down and close their eyes.

2. These seven students then go around and touch one person on the head.

3. Once they all return to the front of the classroom, the teacher says "Heads up, seven up."

4. All the children who have been touched stand up and try to guess who tapped them.

5. If they are right, they must correctly give the answer to a math question on a flash card.

❖ Math Tic-Tac-Toe Bingo

1. For each round, the kids draw a 3 x 3 tic-tac-toe grid on paper.

2. They write one number in each of the nine squares. They must choose numbers between 1–99. Each square must have a different number.

3. The teacher calls out problems with answers of 99 or less. Students cover the squares that match the answers to the problems given. For example, if the teacher calls out "7 x 5," any students who have the number "35" in one of their squares get to cover that number. The first student to get three in a row, just like Tic-Tac-Toe, is the winner.

23	31	5
88	42	16
34	7	80

4. Have the students make a new grid for each new game.

Last-Minute Math Lessons *(cont.)*

❖ Around the World

1. Stand in front of the room with two students. Have them face you.

2. Hold up a flash card, and the first one to say the answer gets to move on to the next spot and challenge the next student.

3. The one who loses sits down wherever he or she is.

4. Only give them one chance. If one child says the wrong answer, the other one gets a chance. If they both miss, they both sit. In that case, go on to the next two kids.

5. The winner is the first one to get back to his seat. This can take a while, but the kids love it.

6. *Hint:* Skip any child who doesn't want to play or can't remain quiet while others are playing.

❖ Drop the Clothespin (or Eraser Basketball)

1. Divide into smaller teams for this game—by rows, groups, etc.

2. Call up one team. Each time a student gets the right answer, he or she gets to drop a clothespin into a jar or throw an eraser into a wastebasket placed several feet away.

3. Let one of your students give out the math facts and another keep score.

4. You just sit back and settle any disputes.

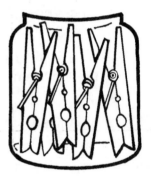

❖ Math Relay

1. Ahead of time, prepare two large grids on the board. The grids can be for counting from 1–100, for example, or they can be multiplication charts.

2. Divide the class into two groups and line the students up facing the board.

3. Each child gets to write in one number, and then he or she goes to the end of the line.

4. If a child sees a mistake, he or she may correct it instead of writing a number.

5. The first team to complete the chart correctly is the winner.

6. There is a "No Talking" rule during this game. Anyone who talks must go to his or her seat.

Math Square

Directions: Have the students cut the squares apart and then put them back together using the numbers as clues.

63 · 9 x 8	6 x 7 · 6 x 9 · 6 x 7	36 · 54 · 6 x 0	0 · 56
72 · 7 x 7 · 40	42 · 49 · 24 · 9 x 4	9 x 6 · 6 x 4 · 45 · 9 x 7	7 x 8 · 5 x 9 · 27
8 x 5 · 28 · 48	36 · 7 x 4 · 6 x 5 · 9 x 5	63 · 30 · 5 x 5 · 8 x 8	9 x 3 · 25 · 81
8 x 6 · 7 x 3 · 9 x 8	45 · 21 · 6 x 3 · 9 x 8	64 · 18 · 40 · 9 x 8	9 x 9 · 8 x 5 · 9 x 8

Math Challenge

Directions: Have students work individually or in pairs to complete the following problems. Students must show their work from beginning to end.

1. Kelly Jetson works in a model airplane factory. She has found that three out of every 28 planes do not fly straight. If she makes 224 planes, how many will not fly straight?

   _____

2. Troy, Trey, Travis, and Todd are brothers. Troy is half as old as Travis. Travis is three years older than Todd. Todd and Trey together are 17 years old. Trey is eight. What are the ages of all four brothers?

   _____

3. Tim and his friend formed a human pyramid. Each level of the pyramid had one less person than the level below it. If there are six people on the lowest level of the pyramid and only one person on the top of the pyramid, how many people altogether are forming the pyramid?

   _____

4. Complete this pattern: 2, 3, 5, 8, 12, 17, _____, 30, 38, _____, 57, _____, 80

5. Julie loves tulips. In her tulip bed, she has half as many orange as red and four times as many red as yellow. There are two dozen tulips that are either white or yellow. Fifteen are white. How many total tulips does Julie have in the tulip bed?

   _____

6. Mrs. Muro is 29 years old; and her daughter, Nina, is six years old. How old will Nina be when she is half as old as her mother?

   _____

7. The number 12 has six factors (1, 2, 3, 4, 6, 12). That means it has an even number of factors. Find all the numbers from 1–20 that have an odd number of factors. _____

8. Name all of the whole numbers that can be placed in the box so that the total is between nine and 21: (3 x [____]) + 2.

   _____

9. Complete this pattern: 1, 2, 5, 14, 41, _____, _____.

10. Eight people are in a room. If everyone shakes hands with everyone else exactly one time, how many handshakes will there be in total? Draw a picture or make a list. _____

Math Challenge

Answer Key

1. If a ratio is created so that 3/28 = x/224, the answer can be found. Twenty-four planes will not fly straight.

2. Start with the information you know: Trey is 8. Therefore, Todd is 9, Travis is 12, and Troy is 6.

3. 21 people. From the bottom up, the layers have 6, 5, 4, 3, 2, and 1. 6 + 5 + 4 + 3 + 2 + 1 = 21

4. Add 1, then 2, then 3, etc., to find the numbers that follow. The three blanks are 23, 47, and 68.

5. Start with the information you know: 15 are white, 9 are yellow, 36 are red, and 18 are orange. Total of 78 tulips.

6. Unless students can create equations, they need to guess and check. In 17 years, Mrs. Muro will be 46 and Nina will be 23.

7. Create a list. 1, 4, 9, and 16 have odd amounts of factors. These are all perfect squares.

8. Guess and check would be the best strategy for students. 3, 4, 5, and 6 all yield an answer between 9 and 21.

9. Triple the number and then subtract one to find the numbers that follow. The two blanks are 122 and 365.

10. A picture, list, or demonstration works the best. 7 + 6 + 5 + 4 + 3 + 2 + 1 + 0 = 28 total handshakes.

Writing Extension: Students will construct five word problems that use at least two mathematical operations (i.e., addition, subtraction, multiplication, division). Students must include the answers to the problems. If time permits, students will share their problems with the class to see if the class can solve them.

Vocabulary Extension: Students must list as many math vocabulary words as they can think of, along with a definition of the word and an example of it. Here is an example:

Vocabulary Word: addition

Definition: the sum of two or more numbers

Example: 2 + 2 = 4

Math Tangram

The tangram is a puzzle originated in China. The set is composed of seven pieces. One piece is a square, another piece is a rhomboid, and the other five pieces are isosceles right triangles of various sizes.

The instructions for playing tangrams are simple and very easy to understand. The objective of the puzzle is to form a figure using the tangram pieces. People find this seven-piece puzzle fascinating and delightful because there are a large variety of ways of putting these pieces together. Using one's own creativity, various tangram figures may be formed. In fact, thousands and thousands of designs have been created over the years just by rearranging these seven tangram pieces. These designs not only include simple geometric shapes like the ones shown below, but also shapes of birds, dogs, cats, and numerous other objects.

Math Tangram Pieces

Cut apart and reassemble the pieces to form the shape of an object.

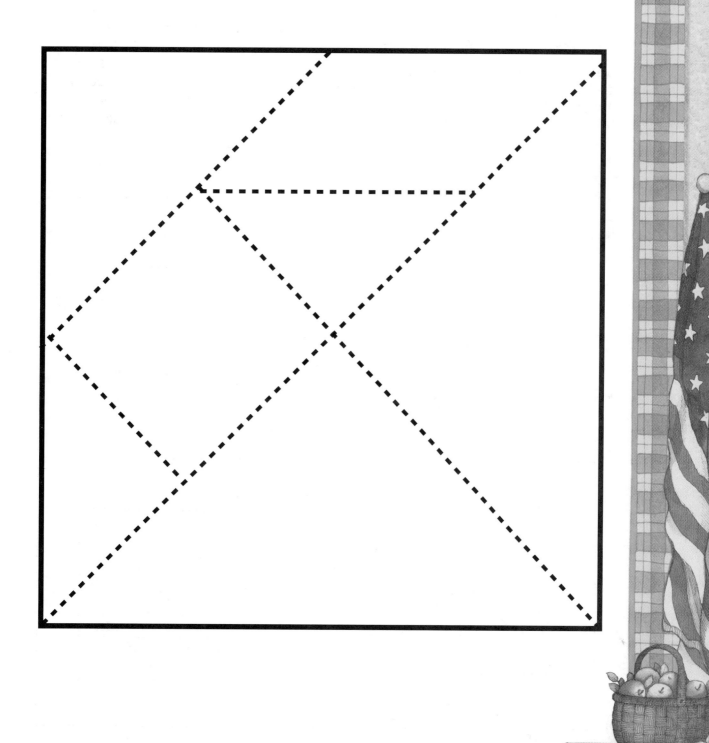

Math Lesson

"Hidden Coin"

Grade Level: primary grades

Time: 15–30 minutes

Objective: Students will find a coin under one of the cups.

Materials: 10 small paper cups, 1 coin

Directions: Label the cups "1st," "2nd," "3rd," etc. Place them upside down. While the students are not looking, place the coin under one of the cups.

Tell the students they are to take turns guessing where they think the coin is. To encourage oral language skills, it is preferable to have the student respond in a full sentence. "I think the coin is under the 3rd cup."

Respond by telling the student, "The coin is under a cup after the 3rd, but before the 8th cup" (if, for example, the coin is under the 5th cup).

Students continue asking questions until the coin is located. When they have had some practice playing the game, they can hide the coin and become the clue giver.

Math Lesson

"Working With Coins"

Grade Level: 2–4

Time: 15–30 minutes

Objective: This activity will help children to develop an understanding of patterns and variables.

Materials: variety of coins

Directions: The class works in small groups of three to four. Have several coins in various denominations available. Come up with a few coin-based questions, such as the following:

- ➥ "I have three coins in my pocket that are worth 12 cents. What are they?"
  (*Answer: 1 dime and 2 pennies*)

- ➥ "I have three coins that are worth 25 cents. What are they?"
  (*Answer: 2 dimes and 1 nickel*).

Have the groups answer quickly. Give them only a few seconds; then take the answers given by the other groups. After each answer, show the group how it is correct.

Then move on to questions that have more than one answer. For example:

- ➥ "I have six coins that are worth 30¢. What are they?"
  (*Answer could be 1 quarter and 5 pennies or 6 nickels.*)

After students are able to answer questions like this, call on groups to make up the questions. This enables them to change the logical reasoning pattern and put your skills to the test!

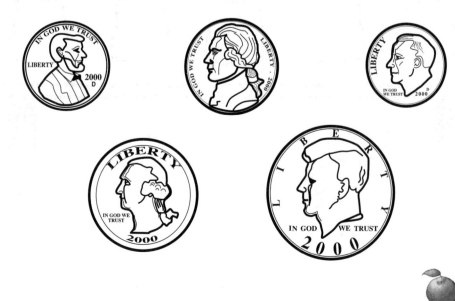

Math Lesson

"Cereal Box Stories"

Grade Level: 2–5

Time: 30 minutes

Objective: Students will use found words to create their own story.

Directions: Give small groups of three to four students a flattened cereal box. One person in the group is designated as the scribe. The groups find words that they like. These might be any words that describe or convince. The scribe writes down between 10–15 words.

Challenge each person in the group to spin a tale that uses whatever number of words you specify (15 for older students and 10 for younger children) from their master list. You can vary the game by suggesting that storytellers use the words in the order they were written, turn the words into characters' names, or place each word at the beginning of a sentence. You can also create a "chain story" by asking each player to build on the previous storyteller's tale.

After about 20–25 minutes working on this assignment, have the students present their stories to the class.

Sample Story

So, did you hear about the young boy named J. Corn Flake whose backyard tree house was fortified with vitamin D and baked fresh daily?

Math Lesson

"I'll Do the Dishes"

Grade Level: upper elementary

Time: approximately 20 minutes

Objective: Practice multiplication and learn the concept of exponential growth

Materials: paper and pencil

Directions: Ask students if they would like to have a job washing dishes (or some other job that adults don't like to do). Tell them they'll be paid one cent the first day, and each day they'll earn twice as much as the day before.

Students work in teams to figure out how much they would earn in two weeks, then a month. If the adult that hires them can still afford them by then, they can hire their own dishwasher at $10 an hour. How much would they earn even after they paid their own employees?

Math Lesson

"Order Off a Menu"

Grade Level: 3–6

Time: 30 minutes

Objective: Students will use found words to create their own story.

Materials: variety of sample menus

Directions: Give small groups of 3–4 students a menu from a local restaurant. One person in the group is designated as the scribe. The groups find dishes that they like and want to order. These might be for one or more people. The scribe writes down between 4–10 different foods.

The small groups order meals for one or more persons; write down the food; and on a separate piece of paper, write the costs for the food and drinks. They pass this to another group and they, in turn, figure out the final cost.

After everyone has had an opportunity to do this in small groups, try a variation where everyone figures their own meal and calculates the tip, tax, change received back, or exact bills and coins needed to pay for their orders.

Science Lesson

"Mystery Bag"

Grade Level: primary grades

Time: 35–40 minutes

Objective: Improve observation, inference, and communication skills

Materials: paper bag and objects(s) to put in bag

Directions: Place any object in a paper bag. Make a simple chart on the board by writing the words "yes" and "no" and drawing a dividing line down the middle.

This activity is conducted with the whole class.

Allow different children to ask questions about the characteristics of what they think might be in the bag. For example, "Is it black?" "Does it have four eyes?" or "Can you bounce it?" Place correct responses under the "yes" column and incorrect responses under the "no" column. After the three responses, read what has been written so far before continuing.

When the students have at least three good clues under the "yes" column, say, "Now it is time for guessing what is in the bag." If no one guesses correctly, ask for more clues and continue.

If a student guesses correctly, hold up the object and read the clues again to the class to see if they match the object.

Continue the lesson by allowing a student to put in the next object and assist the teacher in answering the questions.

Science Lesson

"Jelly-Side Down"

Grade Level: high school

Time: one class period

Objective: Students conduct a controlled experiment.

Background Information: Controlled experiments are based on the comparison of a control group with an experimental group. The control group and the experimental group are identical except for the one factor being tested for in the experiment. This factor is called the *independent variable*. The independent variable is the factor in an experiment that the scientist changes or manipulates. The dependent variable is the factor that changes as a result of what the scientist does to the independent variable. Controlled experiments usually change only one variable at a time, so the scientist knows what is being changed and what is being tested. Information, called *data*, is collected as the experiment is completed. After completing an experiment, the scientist analyzes the data. Conclusions about the posed question are then drawn from the analyzed data.

Materials: several slices of plain white bread for each student or cooperative group in class, jelly, butter knife, tape measure, cleaning materials

Directions: Students predict what will happen when a piece of jellied bread is dropped off a table. From these observations, students pose a question concerning which side of the jellied bread will land on the floor. Students then design experiments to probe the prediction. The experiments are completed, data collected and conclusions drawn. Finally, each student writes a report to persuade others of the validity of his or her experimental conclusion.

Science Lesson

"Biology Mural Project"

Grade Level: high school

Time: one class period

Objective: Students working in small groups choose a selection of the most important concepts and/or terms in a unit of study. After discussion and elimination, the group decides on the most important terms/concepts. These terms are then used to develop a concept map with one overlying theme. From this concept map, the students construct a mural which is to be displayed in the halls of the school or other appropriate place. This activity forces students to decide on the major concepts and come to an agreement within the group as to the relevance and relationships of the concepts. They must then cooperate to create a mural that will convey their message with a minimum of words.

Materials: markers, crayons, or other paint medium; poster board, butcher paper (or any available paper)

Directions: On a 4" x 6" foot piece of newsprint, students will measure, cut off, and design a mural illustrating the concepts that they have found to be important in the current unit.

1. They are to show a relationship between the concepts of this unit using drawings and very few words.

2. Grade will be determined by the following criteria: accuracy of concept relationships, completeness of project, creativity in expression, the amount of contribution that each student makes to the group effort, and punctuality.

3. They may work with up to three others in a group. They will complete a peer evaluation form assessing each student contribution to the group, as well as the other members' contribution.

Assessment: Students will be evaluated using a scoring rubric on a teacher-developed project assessment form and peer evaluation form, which stresses completeness of idea, ability to connect ideas, neatness, ability of group to work together, and uniqueness of presentation.

Science Lesson

"The Cell"

Grade Level: high school

Time: one class period

Objective: This lesson is designed to help students visualize plant and animal cells, understand the parts of a cell and their functions, and distinguish plant cells from animal cells. Students will do this by completing a three-fold task:

1. Researching the function of their assigned cell part.

2. Drawing and cutting out their assigned cell part.

3. Presenting their information to the class and placing their cell part on the classroom animal and plant cells.

At the end of this activity, students will see a homemade plant and animal cell. They will understand the parts of a cell and their functions by the research they conducted and from the information they gathered from listening to their peers. They will be able to visually see the difference between plant and animal cells and will have written the differences down in their notes.

Materials: two pieces of butcher paper (one for the plant cell and one for the animal cell), white paper (to make their drawings), markers (to color their drawings), scissors (to cut out their drawings)

Science Lesson

"The Cell" (cont.)

Directions: The cell theory tells us that the cell is the basic unit of life, all organisms are made up of cells, and new cells come only from other living cells. Whether you are a simple organism made up of only one cell (such as an amoeba) or a complex organism made up of many cells (such as a human), each cell is built the same way. A single cell works like a fast-food restaurant. There are many important jobs to be done to get an order out to the customer, such as someone to make the French fries, someone to cook the hamburgers, someone to prepare the sandwiches, someone to prepare the drinks, someone to take the order, etc. In order for a cell to work as efficiently, there are many cell parts that must work together. Cells can also work together to perform some complicated functions. For example, cells work together to form muscle tissue, which aids in movement. But before we can understand these complicated functions, we must understand the functions of the cell and its parts.

Each group will be assigned a cell part(s). Each group will find the following information about their cell part:

1. Determine whether the cell part(s) belong in a plant cell, an animal cell, or both.

2. Write the function(s) of the cell part(s).

3. Draw and cut a picture of your cell part for both the plant and animal cell. If the cell is equipped with more than one of your cell parts, then you need to draw and cut out the appropriate number of cell parts for each cell. Be sure to notice the size of your plant and animal cells. Make sure that your cell part is the appropriate size.

Each group will present their cell part(s) to the class. Each member of the group must participate in the presentation. During the presentation, explain the information your group researched; then place your cell part(s) on the butcher paper in the appropriate place for both the plant and animal cell. Each group will be assigned one of the following cell parts:

- nucleus
- endoplasmic reticulum and ribosomes
- mitochondria and ATP
- chloroplast and chlorophyll (you will draw your structures directly on the butcher paper)
- cell membrane and cell wall
- cytoplasm, protoplasm, and vacuole

Last-Minute Science Lessons

❖ Successful Failures

Writing Situation: When Thomas Edison invented the light bulb, he tried more than 2,000 experiments before he got it to work. A young reporter asked him how it felt to fail so many times. Edison said, "I never failed. I invented the light bulb. It just happened to be a 2,000-step process."

Directions for Writing: Students are to write about a time that they failed at something when they first attempted it—and how they kept at it, improved, and eventually succeeded.

❖ Underwater Lab

Writing Situation: Underwater labs have existed for about 30 years. The purpose of the habitats thus far has been to enable scientists to conduct undersea research. Hydrolab has operated since 1970 in the Caribbean. Another habitat, called the Western Regional Undersea Laboratory (WURL), is planned for the waters off Catalina Island, California.

Directions for Writing: Brainstorm about the requirements for undersea living and working (oxygen, food, space, movement, water pressure, etc.). Draw a picture of your idea of an undersea laboratory. In an essay, describe your picture in detail. (This lesson can be done as a cooperative group activity, depending on how well behaved and cooperative the class is.)

Last-Minute Science Lessons *(cont.)*

❖ Water Everywhere

Writing Situation: Have the following questions on an overhead with the answers (in parentheses) hidden.

1. How much of Earth's water is freshwater? (3%)

2. How much of Earth's total freshwater is available for human consumption? (1%)

3. Where is the greatest amount of fresh water on Earth? (the polar icecaps, which contain 6 million square miles of water—enough to feed all the world's rivers for 100 years)

4. How much water does the average American use in a day? (200 gallons)

5. What percent of a living tree is water (75%)

6. What percent of your brain is water? (75%)

7. How much of an adult body is water? (65–70%)

8. How much water is needed to produce a Sunday newspaper? (150 gallons)

Directions for Writing: Discuss answers. Then have students write an essay on the importance of water in their lives and how they can conserve it.

❖ Brainstorming Experiment

Situation: List the following brainstorming prompts on the board. Give time parameters for each category (3 minutes if doing individually; 5–7 minutes if doing as a group).

1. List all the foods that you can think of that are yellow.

2. List all the pieces of science equipment you have used this year or seen in a movie in class this year.

3. List different types of scientists.

4. List all the ice-cream flavors you can recall.

Directions: Stop after each category and have one student or group share their list, while other students are checking off items listed. The next student or group will share on those items that haven't already been listed. You can have overall winners by group or individual. For more items, give any science-related category for the class to brainstorm.

Great Science Tricks

◦• Egg in a Bottle

Materials: hard-boiled egg (peeled); paper; match or lighter (to be used by teacher or other adult); large glass bottle

How: Get a hard-boiled egg and peel the shell off. Next, light a bunch of paper on fire and, as it's burning, toss it into a glass bottle. Then, place the egg on top of the bottle, much like a cork. Now the egg should start to gradually slide down the bottle.

Why: The air in the bottle gradually becomes denser, and the air pressure in the bottle will greatly decrease. Due to the atmospheric pressure, the egg will be forced to travel down the neck of the bottle, hugging it tightly.

◦• Candle-Blowing Bottle

Materials: empty wine bottle, candle, match or lighter (to be used by teacher or other adult)

How: Take an ordinary wine bottle and cover the top opening with the ball of your left hand. Now slightly open one side so just a little crack is showing. Blow into it as hard as you can for several seconds. Quickly close the opening. Next, hold the bottle so that the opening is an inch away from a lit candle's flame; and, at an angle, move your hand so that there is a slight opening. The air that is trapped inside will come out in a small gush of wind. If it's strong enough, it might even blow the flame out.

Why: The air that you trapped inside the bottle is compressed. It is much like the machine at gas stations that can fill your bike or car's tires with air.

◦• The Immovable Coin

Materials: cardboard (5" x 5"), coin (a quarter works best)

How: First, you need to cut a piece of cardboard paper that is 5" x 5". Place this piece on the tip of your index finger. Next, place a quarter onto the paper, centered right above your finger. Now give the paper a fast, sharp flick. The coin should stay on your finger!

Why: The coin will be indifferent to the loss of its support.

150

Last-Minute Science Lessons *(cont.)*

⊷ The Remote-Control Soda Can

Materials: soda can, balloon

How: Put a soda can on its side on any flat surface. Blow up a balloon and rub it back and forth across your hair really fast. Hold the balloon about an inch in front of the can and watch it start to roll—even without you touching it. Move the balloon away from the can slowly and the can will follow.

Why: With this experiment you are piling up electrons on one thing and using them to attract the protons in something else. When you rub a balloon on your hair, it ends up loaded with electrons. Those electrons can attract the protons in a soda can, the protons in a trickle of water, the protons in your hair, or the protons in a wall.

⊷ The Water Candlestick

Materials: candle stub, bowl, water, nail, match or lighter (to be used by teacher or other adult)

How: Have a deep bowl full of water ready. Light a candle stub, and then get a nail and heat it up on the candle's flame. Jab the nail into the middle of the candle (it can't interfere with the wick, though). Now place the candle into the bowl of water—the candle top should be even with the water. The cool thing is, the candle should burn so that it is hollow!

Why: The heating effect was cooled by the opposite effect of the water.

⊷ Crystals on a Thread

Materials: two paper cups, baking soda, water, yarn, red chili bean, pencil

How: Dissolve baking soda in water. When the crystals no longer vanish despite repeated stirring, you can be certain that the solution is saturated. Now put the liquid into a different cup. Take a piece of yarn and tie a red chili bean to one end. Tie the other end to a pencil. Set the end with the bean into the liquid and lay the pencil across the top. (Make sure that the yarn is at the right length so that the bean isn't touching the bottom of the cup.) A crystal structure should start growing on the bean after a while.

Why: The bean absorbs water and swells, but only the water is absorbed. The dissolved soda is "kicked out" and attaches itself to the outside of the bean in form of crystal needles. The more water it absorbs, the more soda is rejected, and so it forms even more crystals.

Social Studies Lesson

"Hidden Treasure"

Grade Level: primary grades

Time: one class period

Objective: This activity gets the students to relate to the characters in the story or text by connecting what they read to their lives.

Materials: various objects

Directions: Read a book to kick off a unit of study to create a rich context and build background knowledge many children need in order to understand their social studies textbook. Show the artifact replicas to enable children to raise questions and set a purpose for their learning. For example, before learning about Benjamin Franklin, show the artifacts and ask, "Why do you think that Benjamin Franklin would have items such as a pen, kite string, and glasses in his pocket?" After children speculate on reasons for the presence of each artifact, they will be eager to discover the links between the objects and his life during the reading.

After this, the teacher asks the students to draw a big pocket and draw objects they might find in the pocket that weren't previously discussed.

Social Studies Lesson

"Change of Venue"

Grade Level: 3–6

Time: 40 minutes

Objective: Students will recreate historical events with new times and dates.

Materials: paper and pencil

Directions: Choose a famous historical event that the students have been studying. Discuss with them where it happened, the event itself, the time period, and the people who were involved. Then select another place with which they are familiar and ask them to retell the tale—this time adjusting the "historical" happening to reflect the change. Older students might want to research the place to add realistic details; younger children can rely on their imaginations or discussions with you to decide which changes might occur. You can provide each player with a different place and see how his or her stories differ.

Alternately, you might choose a change of time instead of place—for example, the French Revolution occurring in the 20th century instead of the 18th century. They can provide all the changed details, such as what the first journalists on the scene reported and what the United Nations intended to do about the fray.

Social Studies Lesson

"Historical Interview"

Grade Level: upper elementary

Time: one class period

Objective: Personalize historical events/people to increase interest and understanding.

Materials: paper, pencil, 3" x 5" index cards

Directions: For this book report, students will need to pick a partner to help them make their oral reports. Each interview book report will be called "A Moment In Time."

Check off each task as you complete it.

❏ The main character you are going to interview is _____.

❏ _____ is the reporter and _____ is the character being interviewed.

❏ Make a commentator card. This is a card telling the commentator how to introduce you. Write this on a 3" x 5" index card. Here is an example:

> "Right now M.I.T.T.V would like to take you back to 1770 to interview one of the most interesting characters in the book *Ben and Me*. Our very own Kim Smith is in Philadelphia, Pennsylvania, live with Ben Franklin. Kim. . . ."

❏ Create an interview. The interview must have a greeting, a minimum of five good questions, and a closing. A good question cannot be answered with a "yes" or "no" or any one-word response. If the person being interviewed answers in one word, ask them if they could please give a few more details.

Example of a greeting:

"Good morning, Ben. Thank you for taking the time to be with us this morning."

Examples of good questions:

"How did you become interested in electricity?"

"What was it like writing the Constitution?"

"Why did you run away to Philadelphia?"

Example of a closing:

"Thank you for your time, Ben. This is Kim reporting live from Philadelphia, Pennsylvania, for M.I.T.T.V. Now back to you, [commentator's name]."

❏ Write down your interview questions on index cards. Rehearse your interview. Be sure your partner can answer all the questions as naturally as possible.

Social Studies Lesson

"Map Quiz"

Grade Level: 5–6

Time: 20 minutes

Objective: Students will use their knowledge of geography to guess names of cities, states, or countries.

Materials: map or globe

Directions: To do this activity, choose a country or continent that the students have studied, then find a map of the place. Next, silently select a city, state, or country. For beginners, you can announce which category it is; for advanced players, you should keep the category a secret, too.

If necessary, offer the children three or more clues to the chosen location. These hints can be simple ("I'm thinking of a state that begins with the letter "V," ends with "A," and is located in a country that begins and ends with "A", or complex ("It's an ancient location, but it's a popular site for modern-day skiers."). Don't forget the zany ("This place is often associated with a very tasty sausage")! You might offer clues related to the place's history, culture, food, dress, or art. Whoever correctly guesses the place gets to create the next geographical riddle.

To increase the challenge for older kids, you might want to provide three "real" clues and one red herring (i.e., a false clue). Turnabout is fair play, though, so if you elect to try this, watch out when it's your turn!

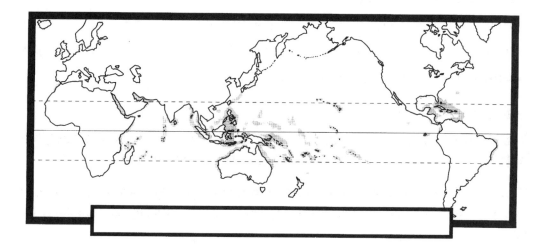

Influential People in History

Name: _____

Here are some of the most influential people in history. Can you connect them with their contribution? An answer key is provided on page 157.

_____ 1. Ts'ai Lun

_____ 2. Johann Gutenberg

_____ 3. Christopher Columbus

_____ 4. Albert Einstein

_____ 5. Louis Pasteur

_____ 6. Galileo Galilei

_____ 7. Aristotle

_____ 8. Euclid

_____ 9. Moses

_____ 10. Charles Darwin

_____ 11. Shih Huang Ti

_____ 12. Augustus Caesar

_____ 13. Karl Marx

_____ 14. Orville and Wilbur Wright

_____ 15. George Washington

_____ 16. James Watt

_____ 17. Martin Luther

_____ 18. Thomas Edision

A. Roman ruler

B. created first printing press

C. major prophet of Judaism

D. first president of United States

E. physicist; theory of relativity

F. scientist; pasteurization

G. founder of Communism

H. influential Greek philosopher

I. founder of Protestantism and Lutheranism

J. inventors of modern airplane

K. mathematician

L. inventor of paper

M. inventor of light bulb, phonograph, etc.

N. wrote *On the Origin of the Species*

O. astronomer; described solar system

P. explorer; led Europe to Americas

Q. developed the steam engine

R. Chinese emperor

Influential People in History

Answer Key

1. Ts'ai Lun = inventor of paper (L)

2. Johann Gutenberg = created first printing press (B)

3. Christopher Columbus = explorer; led Europe to Americas (P)

4. Albert Einstein = physicist; theory of relativity (E)

5. Louis Pasteur = scientist; pasteurization (F)

6. Galileo Galilei = astronomer; described solar system (O)

7. Aristotle = influential Greek philosopher (H)

8. Euclid = mathematician (K)

9. Moses = major prophet of Judaism (C)

10. Charles Darwin = wrote *On the Origin of the Species* (N)

11. Shih Huang Ti = Chinese emperor (R)

12. Augustus Caesar = Roman ruler (A)

13. Karl Marx = founder of Communism (G)

14. Orville and Wilbur Wright = inventors of the modern airplane (J)

15. George Washington = first president of United States (D)

16. James Watt = developed the steam engine (Q)

17. Martin Luther = founder of Protestantism and Lutheranism (I)

18. Thomas Edison = inventor of light bulb, phonograph, etc. (M)

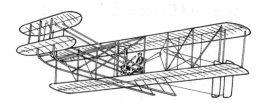

The United States

Directions: Look at the numbers written on the states in the map. Next to each state name below, write the number that corresponds to that state on the map.

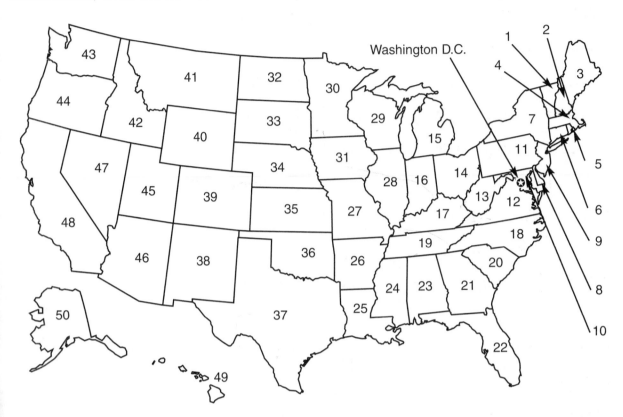

Alabama _____

Alaska _____

Arizona _____

Arkansas _____

California _____

Colorado _____

Connecticut _____

Delaware _____

Florida _____

Georgia _____

Hawaii _____

Idaho _____

Illinois _____

Indiana _____

Iowa _____

Kansas _____

Kentucky _____

Louisiana _____

Maine _____

Maryland _____

Massachusetts _____

Michigan _____

Minnesota _____

Mississippi _____

Missouri _____

Montana _____

Nebraska _____

Nevada _____

N. Hampshire _____

N. Jersey _____

N. Mexico _____

N. York _____

North Carolina ___

North Dakota ___

Ohio _____

Oklahoma _____

Oregon _____

Pennsylvania _____

Rhode Island _____

South Carolina ___

South Dakota ___

Tennessee _____

Texas _____

Utah _____

Vermont _____

Virginia _____

Washington ___

West Virginia ____

Wisconsin _____

Wyoming _____

The United States

Answer Key

Alabama = 23	Montana = 41
Alaska = 50	Nebraska = 34
Arizona = 46	Nevada = 47
Arkansas = 26	New Hampshire = 2
California = 48	New Jersey = 9
Colorado = 39	New Mexico = 38
Connecticut = 6	New York = 7
Delaware = 8	North Carolina = 18
Florida = 22	North Dakota = 32
Georgia = 21	Ohio = 14
Hawaii = 49	Oklahoma = 36
Idaho = 42	Oregon = 44
Illinois = 28	Pennsylvania = 11
Indiana = 16	Rhode Island = 5
Iowa = 31	South Carolina = 20
Kansas = 35	South Dakota = 33
Kentucky = 17	Tennessee = 19
Louisiana = 25	Texas = 37
Maine = 3	Utah = 45
Maryland = 10	Vermont = 1
Massachusetts = 4	Virginia = 12
Michigan = 15	Washington = 43
Minnesota = 30	West Virginia = 13
Mississippi = 24	Wisconsin = 29
Missouri = 27	Wyoming = 40

A Citizenship Test

The United States has always been open to those who want to make it their home. In 2000, 888,788 men, women, and children pledged their new allegiance to the flag of the United States of America. To take the test you must be at least 18 years old; be lawfully admitted to the United States for permanent residence; and have the ability to speak, read, and write the English language.

The following questions come from the Immigration and Naturalization Service Web site and mirror the actual test.

1. Who elects the president of the United States? _____

2. What is the introduction to the Constitution called? _____

3. How many times may a Senator be re-elected? _____

4. How many changes or amendments are there to the Constitution? _____

5. What special group advises the president? _____

6. What makes up the executive branch of our government? _____

7. Who designed the Declaration of Independence? _____

8. Who becomes president if the president should die? _____

9. Which branch of the government interprets laws? _____

10. Which branch of the government writes laws? _____

11. Which branch of the government executes laws? _____

12. Who selects the Supreme Court justices? _____

13. Who becomes president if both the president and vice president die? _____
_____

14. How many states are there in the United States? _____

15. Which president was the first commander in chief of the United States Army and Navy? _____

16. In what year was the Constitution written? _____

17. What were the original states of the United States called? _____

18. What ship did the pilgrims use to come to America? _____

19. What was the last state to join the United States? _____

20. Who was "The Father of our Country?" _____

21. Who was president during the Civil War? _____

22. How old must you be to vote in the United States? _____

23. Who wrote "The Star-Spangled Banner"? _____

24. What holiday was celebrated for the first time by American colonists?
_____

25. How many Supreme Court justices are there? _____

A Citizenship Test
Answer Key

1. The Electoral College

2. The Preamble

3. There is no limit.

4. 27

5. The cabinet

6. The president, cabinet, and departments under the cabinet

7. Thomas Jefferson

8. The vice president

9 Judicial

10. Legislative

11. Executive

12. The president

13. The speaker of the House of Representatives

14. 50

15. George Washington

16. 1787

17. The colonies

18. The *Mayflower*

19. Hawaii

20. George Washington

21. Abraham Lincoln

22. 18

23. Francis Scott Key

24. Thanksgiving

25. 9

Last-Minute Drama Lesson

❖ Role Playing

Directions: Distribute three index cards (or pieces of paper) to each student. On one card, write a job that a person could have (such as a dentist, cab driver, basketball player, etc.). On the next card, write a location (such as a bus stop, restaurant, etc.). On the third card, write a characteristic (such as "crazy," "shy," "frightened," "angry," etc.).

| astronaut | football field | excited |

Keep the cards in three piles and mix them up. Select partners. One pair of partners comes up to the front of the room. Each partner selects a card from each pile. He or she looks at the cards but does not show anyone else the cards that have been drawn. The cards are given to the teacher. Each partner begins a scene with improvised dialogue. Have the class guess the situation.

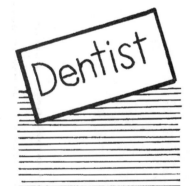 

Dentist BusStop Shy

Last-Minute Music Lesson

❖ Musical Words

Directions: Make a list of ten of the last names of musicians, composers, musical instruments, or notation names (e.g., Mozart, trumpet, staff). Do not show your list to anyone else. Students number off. Student one writes a name on the board. Student two selects a name to intersect or attach to the first word. The student who is next continues in the style shown below, intersecting or attaching each word as he or she takes a turn. A grid drawn in a different color is helpful.

Use a dictionary to find the definition and description of musical instruments. Use instruments found in the woodwind, brass, string, and percussion families, as well as lesser-known old instruments. A simple sketch of the instrument may be included, too. After students have completed the task, read a definition and see if anyone can identify the instrument. This can be played as a game.

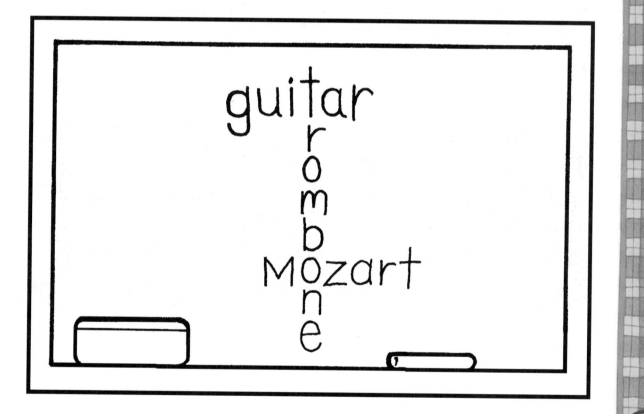

Using the Newspaper

The newspaper is an endless source of great teaching opportunities. Many newspapers even have a section telling the teacher how best to use the articles included. Here are some ideas and how they might be used.

Things to Be Careful of When Using Newspapers

✗ Be sure to look at what is on the back of the newspaper page. Check for inappropriate materials, such as underwear ads, scandalous stories, etc.

✗ It's best if you give each child a piece of newsprint no bigger than the size of his or her desk.

✗ Don't allow students to spread the paper all over the floor. This becomes slippery and may be dangerous or used as a place to play.

✗ The newspaper is written at about 5th grade level. Remember this so you don't expect the younger children to be able to read it with more success than is possible.

Math Activities

- Using the classified ads, compare the price for one-bedroom apartments in your area.

- Add up the prices advertised from one store. Add up the prices from another store and compare which store might be the best value.

- Buy a product you see advertised and write a letter to your parents telling them why it is such a good deal.

- Plan a meal from the food advertised and add up the total bill. For an extension activity, figure out the tax on your purchase.

- Go shopping for a car. What is the best buy you've found? Why is it better than the other cars advertised?

Science Activities

- Chart the weather.

- Find an article about a scientific topic and report on it.

- Find an article that includes some mention of specific plants or rock formations.

- Report on an article that shows a new invention or the direction technology may go in the future.

Using the Newspaper *(cont.)*

Letters and Words

- Using a yellow crayon, highlight the vowels in each word.
- Using a red crayon, underline any descriptive words you see.
- Find every letter of the alphabet and highlight each.
- Hunt for nouns and tell which kind they are (person, place, thing, idea).
- Hunt for verbs and tell which kind they are (action or being).
- Hunt for your spelling words.
- Hunt for words with 1, 2, 3, etc., syllables.

Writing

- Using a red crayon, mark the indentation of every paragraph.
- Highlight the "main idea" sentence in each paragraph.
- Write a paragraph to insert in an article.
- Remove every fifth word and let someone else substitute their own thoughts. Compare with the original.
- Write a follow-up article to something you have read.
- Write a letter to the editor expressing a point of view on an issue that interests you.

Current Events

- Read an article and prepare a short report about an event.
- With sticky notes on a wall map, show where the events are happening.
- Find stories that occur on each continent.
- Find and report on a story where a child is involved.
- Find someone in the paper who is facing a problem and tell how you would solve it.

Comics

- Using Sunday comics, erase or white-out the captions. Now write your own.
- Draw your own version of your favorite cartoon, adding what you think the characters might do.
- Write a letter to the author of your favorite strip and suggest something funny you think the characters should do.

Great Physical-Education Activities

Do you need something new to offer your classes in the way of physical-education activities? Here's a great resource for games they may not have heard of before.

Tag Games

❖ Six members of the class carry a ball around to tag the other students. Once a student is tagged, he or she must stand still with legs apart and hands on his or her head. To free this person, someone else on his or her team must crawl between his or her legs without being tagged by the ball-carrying member.

❖ In this game, the members play on the basketball court. Three members carry balls to tag the other members. All players must stay on lines, but they can go on any line. Once someone is tagged, he or she then becomes the ball-carrying person.

❖ This is also played on the basketball court. One half of your class is inside, and the other half is lined up outside. One player goes in and has 10 seconds to tag someone. The person tagged then jogs around the court and gets at the end of the line. If no one is tagged in 10 seconds, then the aggressor jogs around the court and gets in line. This moves very fast.

❖ This is a group tag. Scatter your class in a defined area. Start with two players being the "group." They hold hands and run around tagging people with their other hands. Anyone tagged becomes part of the group and can only be tagged with the outside hands. Continue this until everyone is caught or your group is physically exhausted.

❖ This is a game that requires an odd number of people. Players stand back to back with one person "out." After the teacher blows a whistle, everyone runs to a new partner. The "odd man out" also runs to get a partner. The person who is left with no one is now the "odd man out."w

Great Physical-
Education Activities

Tag Games *(cont.)*

❖ Play this game on a basketball court with two "taggers." Give them a soft object to tag other people. The teacher yells out a number between two and five, and the children must get into a group of that number without being tagged. If a student is tagged, he or she becomes "it."

❖ Try this fun tag game: the person who is "it" tries to tag someone on an awkward spot like their back, elbow, or even ankle. The person who is tagged then has to run around with his or her hand on that spot to tag someone else.

❖ This is elbow tag. Couples hook inside elbows and put their outside hands on their hips. The person who is "it" must try to hook their arm through the outside arm of one of the players. When he or she does this, the person on the other side of the group becomes "it."

❖ This tag game is best played inside or on the grass. Six players are chosen to be "it." They carry soft objects, like an eraser, to tag other people. If someone is tagged, he or she then lies stomach down on the floor or grass. To avoid being tagged, a person may lie down on his or her back with feet in the air. If the person is in this position, they may get up at any time and start running around again.

❖ You will need strips of cloth for this tag game. The students will wear them like football flags. The object is for everyone to try to pull out the flags of everyone else. The person with the last remaining flag is the winner. If you want to extend this game, then players get to put their flag back on after resting for 10 seconds.

❖ You will need an even number of students for this one. The players in this game stand about a yard apart, facing each other. One person is the hound, and the other person is designated as fox. When the fox is about to be tagged or is getting tired, he steps between two other players. The person who is facing the fox's back then becomes the hound and chases the former hound.

Great Physical-
Education Activities

Relay Games

❖ **Bowling Relay**

One person runs to a designated spot 20–30 feet away and rolls the ball back to the first person. When the ball crosses the starting line, the next person takes off and does the same thing. The first team with everyone across the line wins the game.

❖ **Over-and-Under Relay**

This is played with the team members in a straight line. The beginning person passes the ball over his or her head, and the second person passes it between his or her legs. The ball continues this way until it reaches the end of the line. For a variation on this game, you can have the last person run to the beginning of the line and continue playing the game.

❖ **Travel Relay**

You start by laying out three hula-hoops or drawing three large circles on the ground. In the first circle, put a jump rope. Place a beanbag in the second circle and a ball in the third circle. The student must run to the first circle, pick up the jump rope, and jump rope to the next circle. There he or she will pick up the beanbag, place it on his or her head, and walk to the next circle. Here he or she will get the ball and bounce it back to the first circle. Finally, the student will run back to the line and tag the next person.

❖ **Guide Relay**

This relay requires that you have a blindfold for each team of two students. One student wears the blindfold, while the other is the guide. The object is to lead the "blind" student, without touching him or her, down to and around the cone and back to the starting line. When they get to the starting line, they must tag the next blindfolded person.

❖ **Stepping Stone Relay**

Each team has four mats or newspapers. The first person must put down the mat, step on it, put down the next mat, and step on it. The object is for the person to step this way across the entire basketball court where he or she is allowed to pick up his or her mat (or newspaper) and run back to where the next person will start doing the same thing.

❖ **Ball Hop Relay**

Try this one with students of any age. They must hop down to the cone and return to the next player holding a ball firmly between their legs. If the ball falls out, it must be replaced on the spot before the player can continue.

Great Physical-Education Activities

Relay Games *(cont.)*

❖ **Cooperative Relay**

This is a cooperative relay where you put the students in teams of six members. Five members hold hands to make a circle, with one person in the middle. As a group, they then run to the opposite side of the basketball court, where at least one member of the team must cross the line. When this happens, they run to the opposite side, where another member crosses the line. When the team crosses a line, they change the person in the middle and take off again. They continue this until everyone has had a chance to be in the middle.

❖ **Line Relay**

Each team of five players is lined up. They put their hands on the person's shoulder in front of them. As a team, they now must run to and around the cone and then back to the starting line. At this time, the person in the front of the team goes to the back and they continue again. They keep doing this until every member is back in his or her original position in line.

❖ **Circle Relay**

Put your students in circles with five or six members. They face outward and hold hands. One person is the driver who faces inward. The object is to drive this team around the cone and back to the starting line. Once you get to the cone, the members will shift so that someone else is the driver. Continue this game until everyone has had a chance to be the driver.

❖ **Pony Express Relay**

For this race, you will need a baton or an eraser for each team of four to six players. Space the team members out around the field, with all the "ones" together, the "twos" together, and so forth. The starting person will run to their next team member and hand off the baton. The new runner will hurry to the next runner and so forth. Continue this game until everyone is back in his or her original position.

❖ **Animal Relays**

These variations can be substituted to any simple tag game making it seem new and exciting:

- ➺ Kangaroo Hop
- ➺ Crab Walk
- ➺ Bear Walk

- ➺ Frog Jump
- ➺ Alligator Crawl
- ➺ Snake Slither

Great Physical-Education Activities

Ball Tricks

❖ The children place the ball in front of them. They jump over the ball then jump backwards over it. Then they will try another variation where they put it beside them and jump sideways over it. Another way to do this is to leap over the ball and back. To make things interesting, they can leap over six balls or jump and twist in the air as they are jumping.

❖ Young children can have fun with this one. They are going to see how many different ways they can hold the ball—up high, down low, in back, between their knees, between their elbows, on the back of their hands, right hand up high, or low reverse. Try something like holding the ball in the right hand while standing on the left foot. Spin the ball on the fingertips. Pass the ball around the body, waist-high, knee-high, or neck-high. Now reverse everything.

❖ Dribbling is fun to do if there is no pressure associated with it. Can you dribble the ball waist-high? Try using your fingertips only. Now dribble with the other hand. Now alternate hands and pass it off in the air. How high or low can you dribble? Turn around in a circle while dribbling. Now turn the other way.

❖ Dribble the ball two minutes without stopping. Change hands while doing this.

❖ Toss the ball in the air, spin around, and catch it on the first bounce. Now try it by spinning around twice and catching it in one hand.

❖ Stand and dribble. As you do this, move to a sitting position, then to your knees, to your stomach, back to your knees, and come back to a standing position.

❖ Hold the ball between your knees. Put one hand in front and one hand in back. Now, switch three times really fast without missing.

❖ Dribble the ball at your side, then change and dribble it under one leg and then the other leg. Keep passing it off five times without missing.

❖ Toss the ball into the air and bounce it off your knee once, then off the ground once and back to your knee. Next try bouncing it off your head, to the ground, and back to your head.

More Great Physical-Education Activities

❖ Find Your Mate

Players are given cards with names of animals on them. Two players in the group will have the same animal. Without making any sounds, they must go around and find their mate by making gestures demonstrating that animal. Sooner or later everyone should be paired up and tell the class what they are. Participants can then show off their gestures.

❖ The Killer Winking Game

In this game, every person receives a card facedown. One of the cards says "Killer" on it. The students put their cards in their pockets and walk around in a designated area. The killer will wink at a person who will then walk 10 steps and fall down in agony. The other players try to figure out who did it. If a person gets it right, the game is over. If that person gets it wrong, then he or she has to fall down, too.

❖ Prudi

In this game, the players close their eyes and walk around. One person is the Prudi and walks around with eyes open. If a student bumps into another student they will ask, "Prudi?" If the other student responds back "Prudi?," then they know they haven't yet found Prudi. If they bump into the designated person, they will get no response. They will then open their eyes and hold hands with that person and become part of Prudi. Continue this until the whole class is holding hands.

❖ Knots

Form a circle with an even number of players (between 8–12). Students should take the hand of another person who is not standing next to them. When everyone in the group is holding someone's hands they are to hold on and begin turning their bodies and unraveling until they are all untangled and back in the circle holding hands. Some may be standing backwards, while others are forwards.

More Great Physical-
Education Activities

❖ Group Juggling

Players get in a circle and one person throws an object (such as a ball or an eraser) to another person. That person turns and throws it to a new person, establishing a pattern around the circle. Person 1 will always throw to person 4. Person 4 will always throw to person 6, and so forth. While this is going, introduce a second object and continue the same pattern at the same time. You can do this until you have about four or five objects flying through the air.

❖ Snake in the Grass

Set your boundaries in a grassy area. One person lies on his or her stomach and pretends to be a snake. The other people crowd around to touch the snake with one finger. When the teacher shouts "Snake in the Grass," everyone runs within bounds of the snake area, while the snake, crawling on his or her belly, tries to touch them. If a person is touched, he or she then becomes a snake. The last person to be touched becomes the snake in the new game.

❖ Volley Dodge Ball

Arrange half of the players on the outside of a square or circle, while the others are inside. Students will try to get others out by serving the ball underhand (as they would in volleyball). When a player is hit, the striker exchanges places with the hit player. Keep six or seven balls going.

❖ Bowling Dodge Ball

This game is the same as Volley Dodge Ball, except that the players on the outside bowl the ball instead of throwing it.

❖ Pinball Dodge Ball

Again, this game is the same as the other Dodge Ball games, except that the players on the outside must turn around and shoot the ball back through their legs at the center players.

More Great Physical-Education Activities

❖ **Head-and-Tail Dodge Ball**

Choose eight players for the center. These players will pair up with the back person putting his or her hands on the front player's waist. The object of the game is to hit the tail with the ball. When this happens, the tail becomes the head, the head joins the outside circle, and the person who threw the ball becomes the tail.

❖ **Donkey Dodge**

This is the same game as the one above, except you have three players hooked together. When the tail is hit, they move up, the head moves out, and the striker becomes the new tail.

❖ **National Ball**

Use a volleyball or basketball court to play this game. Put your players into two teams. The object is to hit a player on the opposite team so he or she is out. When a person is out, that person goes to the opposite end of the court from his or her team and continues to play by throwing the ball at the opposing team. The team with the last person in is the winner.

❖ **Pin Boundary Ball**

Again, use a volleyball or basketball court to play this game. Each team begins with 3, 4, 5, or 6 balls. On signal, they attempt to roll the ball across their opponent's end zone area. If it goes across this area, they get a point. The opposing team may not touch the ball once it goes into this end zone.

❖ **Buddy Spud**

The class gathers in the middle of a circle. Players are numbered into five or more groups with four players in each group. Number them 1111, 2222, 3333, and so forth. Have all the 1's throw the ball in the air while you call out the number of one of the groups (e.g., 6). Those people catch the balls while everyone else runs to the outside. The 6's then bowl the ball to the scattered players. The scattered players must leave both feet on the ground as they dodge it. They can turn them on edge, but they can't lift them up. If anyone is hit with the ball, his or her team gets a strike. The team with the least number of strikes wins the game.

Indoor P.E. Games

The following pages offer some great indoor P.E. games. Since you probably will be in a new situation, think through what you expect from the students and what your standards are. How much noise can you and this class handle? Do you have the supplies you need? Will you be able to quiet them down after the activity?

❖ Warm-Up Activities

The following are 3–5 minute activities designed to prepare students for more vigorous movement:

- ➠ Do jumping jacks.
- ➠ Run in place.
- ➠ Lunge with both feet facing forward.
- ➠ Hold one foot behind you with the opposite hand.
- ➠ Touch your toes and hold that position.

❖ Know the Name

1. Draw a grid on the chalkboard.

2. Place a letter in each square.

3. Divide the class into two teams.

4. The first child stands on a designated spot and tosses a beanbag at a square.

5. The child names a famous person, state, or three-syllable word (decide on the rules before starting the game) that starts with that letter.

6. The child writes the word in the appropriate square.

7. A point is given if the child can give a correct response. Another point is given if he or she can spell it right.

❖ Musical Balance

1. The children stand in a circle.

2. They walk around the circle to music you are playing.

3. When the music stops, they look at the teacher, who balances in some way.

4. They assume the same position and balance until the music plays again.

5. If any of the children move any part of their bodies or touch a foot to the floor, they are out.

Indoor P.E. Games *(cont.)*

❖ Quiet Ball

1. All students sit on desks quietly.

2. One student starts by tossing a ball to another student, and so forth, until someone misses.

3. The person who either threw badly or caught badly is out and must sit down.

4. Game continues until all but one person is out.

5. The children only get three seconds to get rid of the ball.

6. If someone talks or if the ball hits the desk, floor, or ceiling, that child is out.

❖ Archery Target

1. Attach a large target to the floor with masking tape.

2. Prepare a set of questions on cards, ranging from difficult to easy, in a certain subject area.

3. The child throws an eraser or beanbag up high above the target.

4. The colors on the target represent subject areas (for example: gold = language; red = science; blue = history, black = math).

5. The child must answer a question according to the color indicated on the target.

6. If the child answers a question correctly, he or she receives a score depending on the color: gold = 9, blue = 7, red = 5, black = 3, and white = 1.

❖ Alphabet Game

1. The children sit in a circle.

2. The first child says the letter "A" and a word that begins with that letter.

3. The next child repeats the letter "A" and the word and says the letter "B" and a word that begins with that letter.

4. The game continues in this manner until all the children have had a turn or all the letters of the alphabet have been named.

Indoor P.E. Games (cont.)

❖ **Paper Plate Balance**

1. The children sit at their desks.

2. Each child has a paper plate balanced on his or her head.

3. One child is designated to call out a direction such as stand up, turn around, or sit down.

4. The members of the class follow the directions.

5. If a plate falls off a child's head, he or she is out of the game.

❖ **Indoor Volleyball**

1. String up a piece of yarn across the room. Teacher may want to hold one end.

2. Students play volleyball using a balloon.

❖ **Tic-Tac-Toe, Five in a Row**

1. Make a large grid on the board.

2. Divide the class into three to four groups.

3. Assign each group a shape.

4. Each group must play tic-tac-toe, placing their shape to win or block.

5. The first team to get five in a row wins the game.

❖ **Dictionary**

1. Divide class into teams of three.

2. Teacher gives each team one new word whose meaning is unknown to the class.

3. One child gives correct meaning to the word, and the other children make up definitions.

4. Class votes on who is telling the truth.

5. A team collects points for every wrong guess by the other team.

Indoor P.E. Games *(cont.)*

❖ Connect the Dots

1. Players start by drawing dots on their page as shown.

2. Players take turns connecting the dots.

3. As players draw the last line to make a square, they put their initial in the square.

4. The player with the most initials in squares is the winner.

❖ Avalanche

1. Designate the corners of the room with the numbers 1–4.

2. One person in the center closes his eyes and counts to 10.

3. Each of the other students runs around the room and settles in one of the corners before the counter says "10."

4. When the counter reaches 10, he or she says "Avalanche" and calls one of the numbers with his eyes still closed.

5. All the people at that corner are out.

6. Start again with the same counter and the people who are still in.

7. Keep playing until one person is left. He or she is the new counter.

❖ Number Spin

1. Prepare 20–30 cards with numbers (e.g., 34, 68, 56).

2. Four or five children stand facing the class.

3. The numbers are pinned or taped to those students' backs.

4. As the teacher claps, the children spin in rapid succession, each briefly showing their number.

5. The last child selects a member from the class to call out the numbers in the order shown.

6. If the child can say the numbers correctly, he or she changes places with the last child in line.

❖ Settling Down

Try some tai chi with a class that needs to settle down. It's easy. Just put on soft music and move your arms and legs very slowly in wide motions. No one is allowed to talk during this exercise. You'll find that it is very calming and a wonderful way to end your activities.

Beginning-of-Class Activities

The first five minutes of a class are among the most critical in teaching for the role they play in setting the instructional stage and transitioning students into lessons. The activities contained on pages 179–214 can serve as great warm-ups to get students into the learning mode.

These activities are flexible enough that they can also be used at other times of the day—for instance, to give you time to grade assignments or to hold students' interest until the lunch or recess bell rings.

Finally, here are some more ideas for keeping the students interested and occupied when you need to find something for them to do. It is important to remember, though, that these ideas are not to take the place of learning; instead, they are to augment it.

- Explore Encyclopedias
- Read a Story
- Draw Pictures
- Make Improvised Music
- Play Hangman
- Make Paper Airplanes
- Play 20 Questions
- Teach Juggling
- Do Word Searches/Crossword Puzzles
- Write and Read Limericks
- Perform Magic
- View Optical Illusions
- Play Bingo
- Do Jigsaw Puzzles

Magic Squares

Thousands of years ago, the Chinese created a fascinating math puzzle called magic squares.

1. Place the numbers 3 through 11 (using each number just once) in the boxes to the right so that any three numbers in a row (across, down, or diagonally) add up to 21.

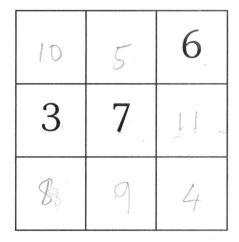

2. Place the numbers 5 through 13 (using each number just once) in the boxes so that any three numbers in a row (across, down, or diagonally) add up to 27.

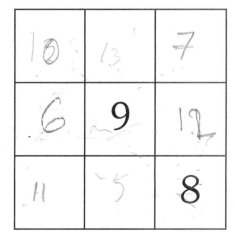

3. Place the numbers 1 through 9 in the boxes so that any three numbers in a row (across, down, or diagonally) add up to 15.

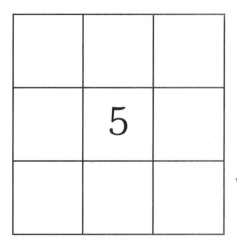

Embedded Shapes

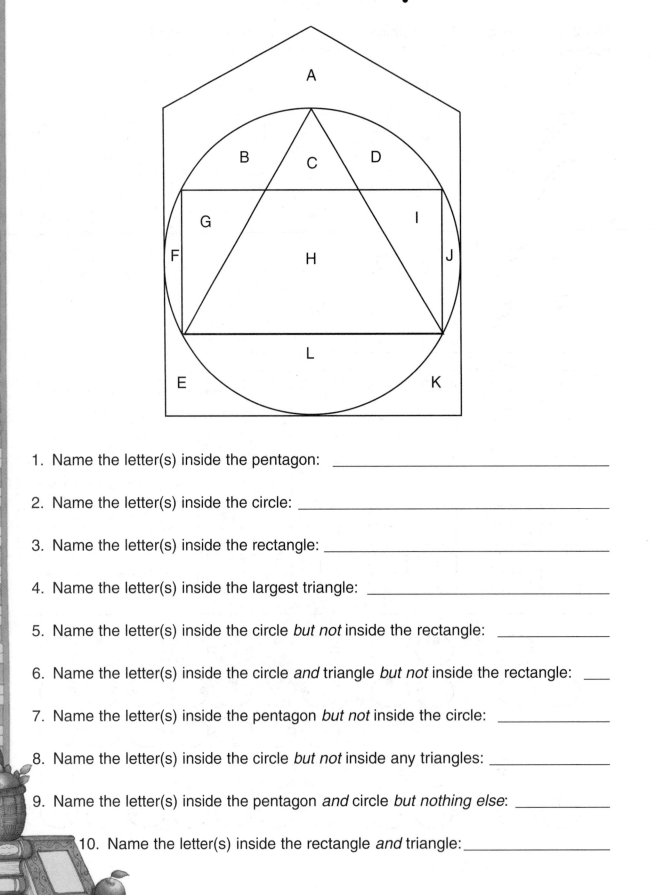

1. Name the letter(s) inside the pentagon: _____

2. Name the letter(s) inside the circle: _____

3. Name the letter(s) inside the rectangle: _____

4. Name the letter(s) inside the largest triangle: _____

5. Name the letter(s) inside the circle *but not* inside the rectangle: _____

6. Name the letter(s) inside the circle *and* triangle *but not* inside the rectangle: ___

7. Name the letter(s) inside the pentagon *but not* inside the circle: _____

8. Name the letter(s) inside the circle *but not* inside any triangles: _____

9. Name the letter(s) inside the pentagon *and* circle *but nothing else*: _____

10. Name the letter(s) inside the rectangle *and* triangle: _____

Groups of Shapes

Match each group of shapes at left with a group at the right. Draw a square around each group that is a match. Write the number in the center. The first one is done for you.

1.   2.

3.   4.

1.   2.

3.   4.

1.   2.

3.   4.

Find the Patterns

Each number line below is divided into equal parts. Fill in the missing numbers.

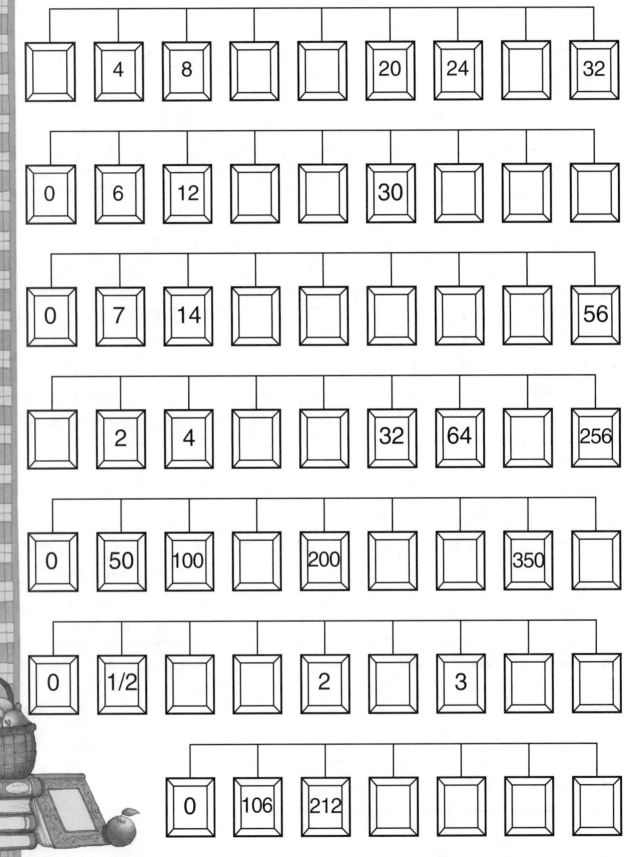

Row 1: ☐, 4, 8, ☐, ☐, 20, 24, ☐, 32

Row 2: 0, 6, 12, ☐, ☐, 30, ☐, ☐, ☐

Row 3: 0, 7, 14, ☐, ☐, ☐, ☐, ☐, 56

Row 4: ☐, 2, 4, ☐, ☐, 32, 64, ☐, 256

Row 5: 0, 50, 100, ☐, 200, ☐, ☐, 350, ☐

Row 6: 0, 1/2, ☐, ☐, 2, ☐, ☐, 3, ☐

Row 7: 0, 106, 212, ☐, ☐, ☐, ☐

Find More Patterns

Find each pattern. Fill in the missing numbers in the row.

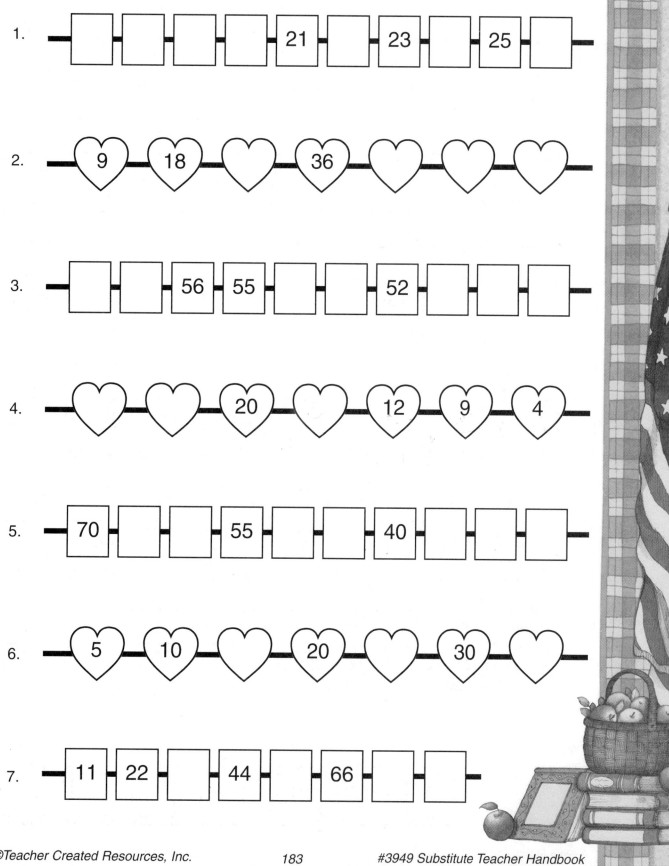

1. ☐ ☐ ☐ ☐ 21 ☐ 23 ☐ 25 ☐

2. 9 18 ♡ 36 ♡ ♡ ♡

3. ☐ ☐ 56 55 ☐ ☐ 52 ☐ ☐ ☐

4. ♡ ♡ 20 ♡ 12 9 4

5. 70 ☐ ☐ 55 ☐ ☐ 40 ☐ ☐ ☐

6. 5 10 ♡ 20 ♡ 30 ♡

7. 11 22 ☐ 44 ☐ 66 ☐ ☐

Follow the Patterns

Continue each pattern.

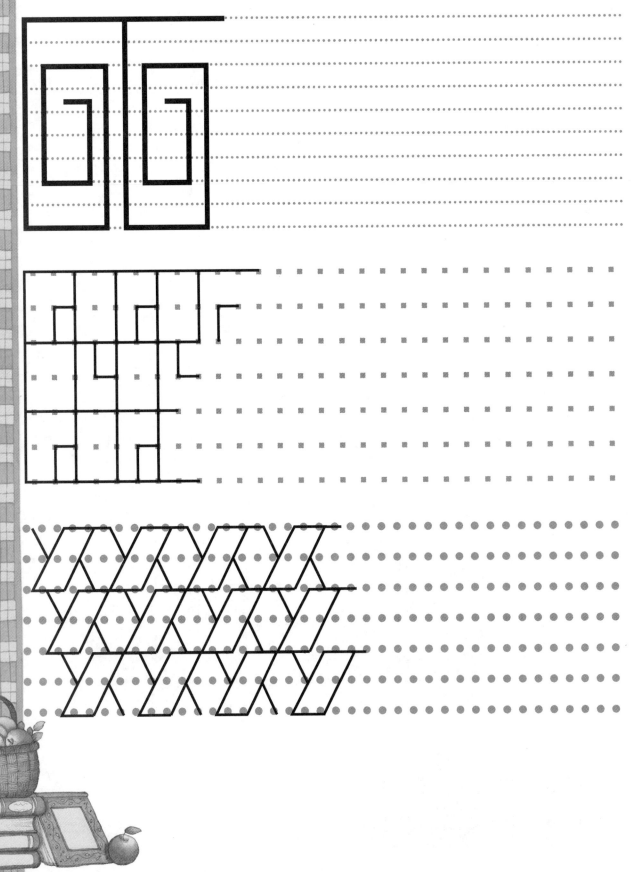

Math and Patterns Activities

Answer Key

Page 179

1.
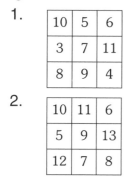

10	5	6
3	7	11
8	9	4

3.

8	3	4
1	5	9
6	7	2

2.

10	11	6
5	9	13
12	7	8

Page 180

1. A, B, C, D, E, F, G, H, I, J, K, L
2. B, C, D, F, G, H, I, J, L
3. G, H, I
4. C, H
5. B, C, D, F, J, L
6. C
7. A, E, K
8. B, D, F, J, L
9. B, D, F, J, L
10. H

Page 181

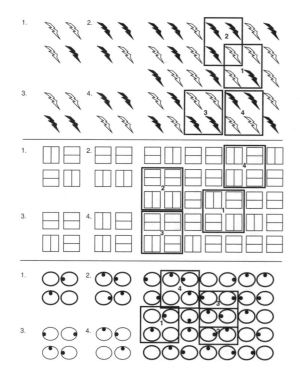

Page 182

1. 0, 12, 16, 28
2. 18, 24, 36, 42, 48
3. 21, 28, 35, 42, 49
4. 1, 8, 16, 128
5. 150, 250, 300, 400
6. 1, 1½, 2½, 3½, 4
7. 318, 424, 530, 636

Page 183

1. 17, 18, 19, 20, 22, 24, 26
2. 27, 45, 54, 63
3. 58, 57, 54, 53, 51, 50, 49
4. 28, 25, 17
5. 65, 60, 50, 45, 35, 30, 25
6. 15, 25, 35
7. 33, 55, 77, 88

Page 184

Drawings should continue the established patterns.

Scrambled Explorers

The names of explorers have been split into two- or three-letter pieces. The letters of the pieces are in order, but the pieces are scrambled. Put the letters together to identify the explorers. Use the clues and the name bank to help you.

1. RO BE ER VE LI RT CA

   ➠ French explorer _____

2. HE AN ES RN RT DO CO

   ➠ traveled west to Baja California _____

3. JU ON EDE AN PO LE NC

   Spanish explorer _____

4. BA OM AS DI EU RT OL

   ➠ explored Africa _____

5. CH LU RI ER CO STO MB US PH

   ➠ started colonies _____

6. IN MU DEC SA HA EL LA MP

   ➠ explored the United States _____

7. HE DS HU NRY ON

   ➠ sailed from Holland _____

8. JA UES RTI CQ CA ER

   ➠ explored Canada _____

9. FR ANC RO CO ZAR IS PI

   ➠ Spanish explorer _____

10. FE ND GEL INA MA RD LAN

    ➠ Has a strait named after him _____

Name Bank

Ferdinand Magellan	Juan Ponce de León
Jacques Cartier	Christopher Columbus
Bartolomeu Dias	Samuel de Champlain
Henry Hudson	Robert Cavelier
Francisco Pizarro	Hernando Cortés

The $100,000 Bill

The $100,000 bill was the biggest bill the U.S. ever made. Only banks used it. So, today the bill is no longer used. Now the $100 bill is the biggest U.S. bill.

Directions: Solve the equations below. Match each answer to a letter from the chart. Put the letters in the boxes to find the answer to the bonus question below.

O = 1479	**I** = 3776	**W** = 4843	**D** = 2219
R = 4873	**L** = 2556	**N** = 3212	**S** = 1245

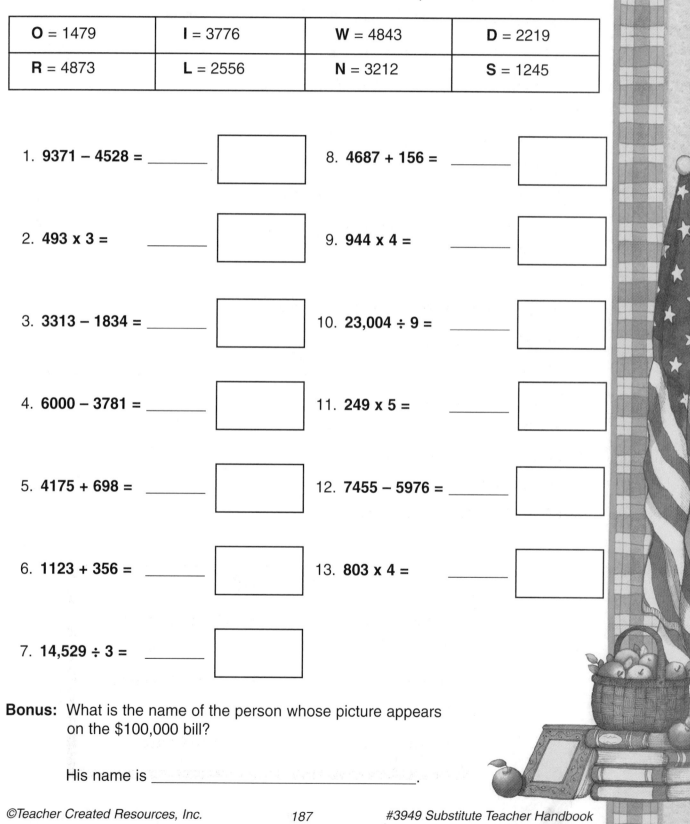

1. **9371 − 4528 =** _____

2. **493 x 3 =** _____

3. **3313 − 1834 =** _____

4. **6000 − 3781 =** _____

5. **4175 + 698 =** _____

6. **1123 + 356 =** _____

7. **14,529 ÷ 3 =** _____

8. **4687 + 156 =** _____

9. **944 x 4 =** _____

10. **23,004 ÷ 9 =** _____

11. **249 x 5 =** _____

12. **7455 − 5976 =** _____

13. **803 x 4 =** _____

Bonus: What is the name of the person whose picture appears on the $100,000 bill?

His name is _____.

Air Accomplishments

Use this code to identify these accomplishments in aircraft. For example, A = 1.

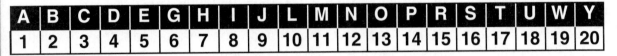

A	B	C	D	E	G	H	I	J	L	M	N	O	P	R	S	T	U	W	Y
1	2	3	4	5	6	7	8	9	10	11	12	13	14	15	16	17	18	19	20

1. These brothers flew short flights in 1903, in North Carolina.

$\overline{19}$ $\overline{15}$ $\overline{8}$ $\overline{6}$ $\overline{7}$ $\overline{17}$

2. This is what airlines were originally developed to carry.

$\overline{18}$. $\overline{16}$. $\overline{11}$ $\overline{1}$ $\overline{8}$ $\overline{10}$

3. Introduced in 1969, this type of plane can carry about 500 passengers.

$\overline{9}$ $\overline{18}$ $\overline{11}$ $\overline{2}$ $\overline{13}$ $\overline{9}$ $\overline{5}$ $\overline{17}$

4. The Montgolfier brothers flew this over Paris in 1783.

$\overline{7}$ $\overline{13}$ $\overline{17}$ $\overline{1}$ $\overline{8}$ $\overline{15}$ $\overline{2}$ $\overline{1}$ $\overline{10}$ $\overline{10}$ $\overline{13}$ $\overline{13}$ $\overline{12}$

5. He flew airmail on the Chicago-to-St. Louis route.

$\overline{3}$ $\overline{7}$ $\overline{1}$ $\overline{15}$ $\overline{10}$ $\overline{5}$ $\overline{16}$ $\overline{1}$.

$\overline{10}$ $\overline{8}$ $\overline{12}$ $\overline{4}$ $\overline{2}$ $\overline{5}$ $\overline{15}$ $\overline{6}$ $\overline{7}$

6. This type of airline service was launched in 1921.

$\overline{17}$ $\overline{15}$ $\overline{1}$ $\overline{12}$ $\overline{16}$ $\overline{3}$ $\overline{13}$ $\overline{12}$ $\overline{17}$ $\overline{8}$ $\overline{12}$ $\overline{5}$ $\overline{12}$ $\overline{17}$ $\overline{1}$ $\overline{10}$

7. In 1936, the DC-3 set a record flying from Los Angeles to here.

$\overline{12}$ $\overline{5}$ $\overline{19}$ $\overline{9}$ $\overline{5}$ $\overline{15}$ $\overline{16}$ $\overline{5}$ $\overline{20}$

8. Samuel P. Langley's airplane in 1896 was powered this way.

$\overline{16}$ $\overline{17}$ $\overline{5}$ $\overline{1}$ $\overline{11}$ $\overline{14}$ $\overline{13}$ $\overline{19}$ $\overline{5}$ $\overline{15}$ $\overline{5}$ $\overline{4}$

9. This is what Boeing is developing to fly at 725 miles per hour.

$\overline{16}$ $\overline{13}$ $\overline{12}$ $\overline{8}$ $\overline{3}$ $\overline{3}$ $\overline{15}$ $\overline{18}$ $\overline{8}$ $\overline{16}$ $\overline{5}$ $\overline{15}$

10. Henri Giffard flew this in 1852.

$\overline{4}$ $\overline{8}$ $\overline{15}$ $\overline{8}$ $\overline{6}$ $\overline{8}$ $\overline{2}$ $\overline{10}$ $\overline{5}$

Social Studies Activities
Answer Key

Page 186

1. Robert Cavelier
2. Hernando Cortés
3. Juan Ponce de León
4. Bartolomeu Dias
5. Christopher Columbus
6. Samuel de Champlain
7. Henry Hudson
8. Jacques Cartier
9. Francisco Pizarro
10. Ferdinand Magellan

Page 187

1. 4843
2. 1479
3. 1479
4. 2219
5. 4873
6. 1479
7. 4843
8. 4843
9. 3776
10. 2556
11. 1245
12. 1479
13. 3212

Bonus: Woodrow Wilson

Page 188

1. Wright
2. U.S. mail
3. jumbo jet
4. hot air balloon
5. Charles A. Lindbergh
6. transcontinental
7. New Jersey
8. steam powered
9. Sonic Cruiser
10. dirigible

Name That Scientist

Directions: Fill in the blanks with the letters to make real words. Use the letters given. When read from top to bottom the letters in a box form a scientist's name. Write the name on the line.

Example:
a [p] e
r [a] n
a [s] k
a [t] e
y [e] t
b [u] t
a [r] t

P a s t e u r

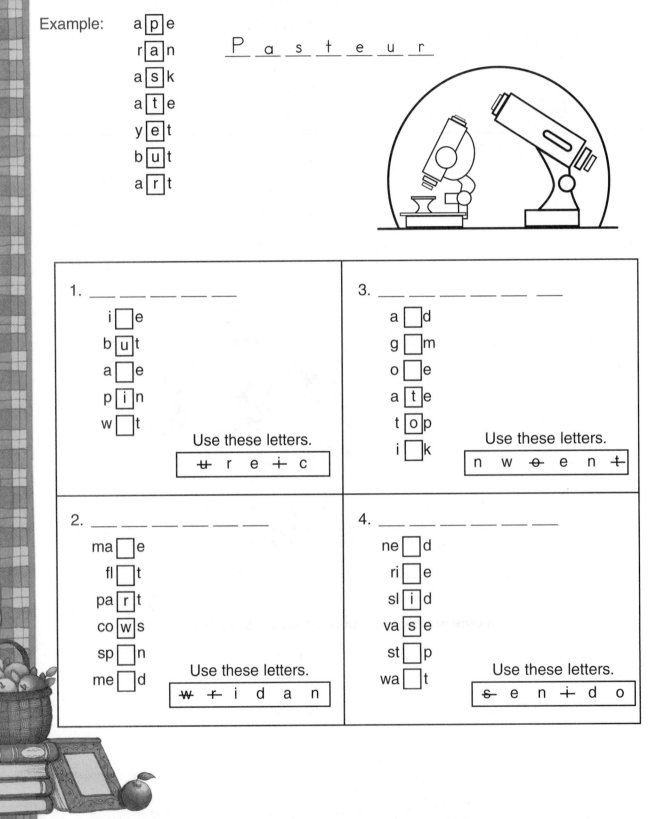

1. ___ ___ ___ ___ ___

i [ ] e
b [u] t
a [ ] e
p [i] n
w [ ] t

Use these letters.
~~u~~ r e ~~t~~ c

2. ___ ___ ___ ___ ___ ___

ma [ ] e
fl [ ] t
pa [r] t
co [w] s
sp [ ] n
me [ ] d

Use these letters.
~~w~~ ~~t~~ i d a n

3. ___ ___ ___ ___ ___

a [ ] d
g [ ] m
o [ ] e
a [t] e
t [o] p
i [ ] k

Use these letters.
n w ~~o~~ e n ~~t~~

4. ___ ___ ___ ___ ___ ___

ne [ ] d
ri [ ] e
sl [i] d
va [s] e
st [ ] p
wa [ ] t

Use these letters.
~~s~~ e n ~~t~~ d o

Windy Weather

1. No wind had been predicted. So when Joyce woke up, she found it startling that a strong wind was blowing. Thinking of the word "startling" made her think of a word puzzle:

   Joyce writes the word "startling." The wind blows one of the letters away (L), leaving behind another word "starting." Then the wind continues to blow one letter away at a time, each time leaving behind a word. The last word has only one letter.

   startling _____

   starting _____

   _____

   _____

   _____

   _____

   _____

   _____

2. Can you change or drop one letter at a time to make "storm" into "gale"? Each step must produce a real word. You must drop one letter before reaching the end. Here's an example of how to solve this type of puzzle:

   front → font → fond → fold → cold

   Now you try:

   storm → _____ → _____ → _____ → _____ → gale

Save the Rain Forest!

You can help to save the rain forest! You found an online site funded by an eccentric billionaire who loves word games. He will purchase and preserve acres of rain forest based on the words you spell using the letters in the word *environmental*. He will buy:

- ↠ **1 acre** for every **4-letter** word
- ↠ **2 acres** for every **5-letter** word
- ↠ **4 acres** for every **6-letter** word
- ↠ **8 acres** for every word with **7 or more letters**

Estimate how many acres of rain forest you can save: _____

environmental

4-letter words	5-letter words	6-letter words	7-letter words
___ x 1 acre = ___	___ x 2 acres = ___	___ x 4 acres = ___	___ x 8 acres = ___

Add the numbers across the bottom row. How many total acres did you save? _____

Science Activities

Answer Key

Page 190

1. Curie

2. Darwin

3. Newton

4. Edison

Page 191

1. startling, starting, staring, string, sting, sing, sin, in, I

2. storm, store, stole, stale, sale, gale

Page 192

There are many correct answers. Here are some suggestions:

Possible 4-letter words: iron, tone, tire, vein, live, liar, vine, line, vain, rain, note, vote, time, nine, tore, more, mail, rail, tail, nail, veil, rate, mate, lean, mean, moan, loan, tear, rent, even, mine, reel, ever, mint, love, move, late, meal, real, mole, mile, evil, tile, near, lent, lame, name

Possible 5-letter words: meant, metal, trial, trail, irate, alive, meter, event, lever, never, leave, train, molar, inner, tidal, vital, valor, manor, viola, ratio, valet, lover, elder, elate, later, vomit, talon

Possible 6-letter words: mental, violet, relive, menial, mantle, antler, reveal, intone, invert, intern, invent, inmate, ration, entire, entail, relate, rental, normal, lament

Possible 7+-letter words: relieve, violent, ornament, violate, lantern, lenient, relative, relation, election, reinvent

Vocabulary Matching I

Directions: Take a look at the **Word Parts** and **Meaning** in the chart. Then use that information to solve the **Matching** section below.

Word Part	Meaning
auto-	self
bio-	life
centri-	center
chrono-	time
crypto-	hidden, secret
geo-	Earth
-gram	something written
-graph	to write

Word Part	Meaning
helio-	the sun
-logy	science or study of
-meter	a device for measuring
moro-	fool
philo-	love of
-phobia	fear, hatred
soph-	wisdom

Matching

_____ 1. autobiography

_____ 2. autograph

_____ 3. biology

_____ 4. chronometer

_____ 5. cryptogram

_____ 6. geology

_____ 7. heliocentric

_____ 8. moron

_____ 9. philosophy

_____ 10. phobophobia

A. one's own signature

B. the fear of fear itself

C. a foolish person

D. the love of wisdom

E. a clock that keeps accurate time

F. the study of Earth

G. something written in secret code

H. the sun as the center

I. the study of life

J. a book written about the author by the author

Vocabulary Matching II

Directions: Take a look at the **Word Parts** and **Meaning** in the chart. Then use that information to solve the **Matching** section below.

Word Part	Meaning
multi-	many
semi-	half
demi-	half
sol-	alone
mill-	thousand

Word Part	Meaning
equi-	equal
hemi-	half
omni-	all
cent-	hundred
kilo-	thousand

Matching

_____ 1. century

_____ 2. demigod

_____ 3. equinox

_____ 4. hemihydrate

_____ 5. kilogram

_____ 6. millipede

_____ 7. multiply

_____ 8. omniscient

_____ 9. semicircle

_____ 10. solitary

A. to increase the amount; to grow in number

B. either of two times in the year when day and night are equal in length

C. half a circle

D. having total knowledge; knowing everything

E. a male being, often the offspring of a deity (god) and a mortal

F. one hundred years

G. a solid containing water in which the molecular ratio of water to anhydrous compound is 1:2

H. existing, living, going without others

I. the base unit in mass; equal to 1,000 grams

J. an insect, supposedly with 1,000 legs

Vocabulary Matching III

Directions: Take a look at the **Latin** and **Greek** prefixes and their **Meanings** in the chart. Then use that information to solve the **Matching** section below.

Latin	Meaning	Greek
uni	one	mon, mono
bi, du	two	di
tri	three	tri
quad(ru), quart	four, fourth	tetr(o)
quin	five	penta
sex(t)	six	hex
sept	seven	hept
oct	eight	oct
non, nov(em)	nine	enne
dec	ten	dec

Matching

_____ 1. biannual

_____ 2. decimeter

_____ 3. duet

_____ 4. monogram

_____ 5. November

_____ 6. pentagon

_____ 7. quarter

_____ 8. quintuplet(s)

_____ 9. trilogy

_____ 10. unique

A. a design composed on one initial

B. happening twice a year or once every two years

C. one-tenth of a meter

D. a group of five offspring born in a single birth

E. a group of two musicians

F. a study of three dramatic or literary works

G. 9th month (of original Roman calendar)

H. one-fourth (of a dollar, etc.)

I. a five-sided figure

J. only one of its kind

Vocabulary Activities

Answer Key

Page 194

1. J
2. A
3. I
4. E
5. G
6. F
7. H
8. C
9. D
10. B

Page 195

1. F
2. E
3. B
4. G
5. I
6. J
7. A
8. D
9. C
10. H

Page 196

1. B
2. C
3. E
4. A
5. G
6. I
7. H
8. D
9. F
10. J

Hidden Meanings

Take a look at the box to the right. Can you guess what it means? Since the word "head" is over the word "heels," it would read, "Head over heels." Get it? Now you try.

Head
Heels

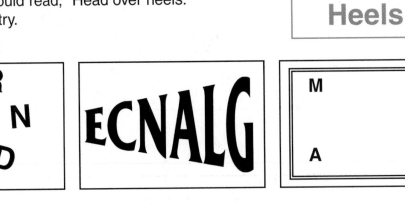

M			E
A			L

1. _____ 2. _____ 3. _____

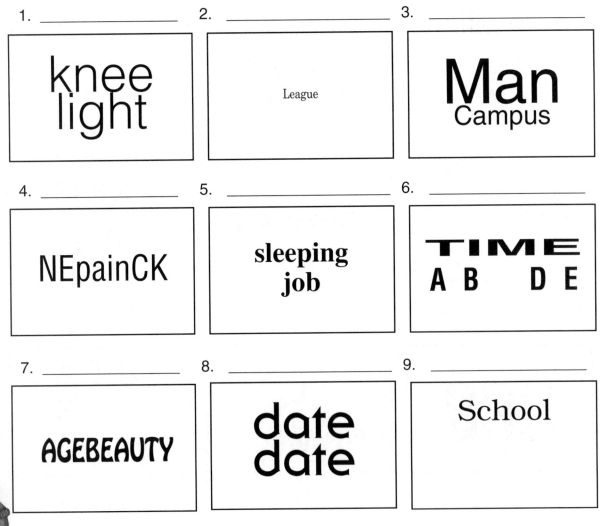

knee
light

League

Man
Campus

4. _____ 5. _____ 6. _____

NEpainCK

sleeping
job

TIME
A B   D E

7. _____ 8. _____ 9. _____

AGEBEAUTY

date
date

School

10. _____ 11. _____ 12. _____

More Hidden Meanings

Explain the meaning of each box.

T A H W (top) M U S T (vertical)	BAN ANA	histalkingsleep
1. _____	2. _____	3. _____
milonelion	eggs / easy	⭕⭕⭕circus
4. _____	5. _____	6. _____
GO IT IT IT IT	nowaysitways	GOOD / EVIL
7. _____	8. _____	9. _____
one one	SLOW (vertical)	S T A N D
10. _____	11. _____	12. _____

Riddle Me This

1. What am I? I am the only thing that always tells the truth. I show off everything that I see. I come in all shapes and sizes. So tell me what I must be!

   _____

2. What happens twice in a week, and once in a year, but never in a day?

   _____

3. Where do you find roads without vehicles, forests without trees, and cities without houses? _____

4. How much wood could a woodchuck chuck if a woodchuck could chuck wood?

   _____

5. What are two things you cannot eat for dinner? _____

   _____

6. What is half of 2, plus 2? _____

7. How many seconds are there in a year? _____

8. When asked what he does all day, a man answered that he sits and makes faces. What does he really mean?_____

   _____

9. What time is it when 12 cats are chasing a mouse?_____

   _____

10. What has a tongue and cannot walk but gets around a lot?

   _____

Riddle Me This (cont.)

1. What goes up and down stairs without moving? _____

   _____

2. Give it food and it will live; give it water and it will die. _____

   _____

3. What can you catch but not throw? _____

4. I run, yet I have no legs. What am I? _____

5. What kind of room has no doors or windows? _____

6. Remove the outside, cook the inside, eat the outside, throw away the inside.
   What is it? _____

7. What can go around the world and still stay in a corner?

   _____

8. What gets wetter the more it dries?_____

9. The more there is of me, the less you see. What am I?_____

   _____

10. They come at night without being called and are lost in the day without being
    stolen. What are they? _____

    _____

ABC Puzzlers

Each equation below contains the initials of words that will make the statement correct. Find the missing words.

Examples:

9 P in the SS = _____ nine planets in the solar system _____

3 BM, SHTR = _____ three blind mice, see how they run _____

5 D in a ZC = _____ five digits in a zip code _____

1. 26 L in the A _____

2. 52 W in a Y _____

3. TE invented the LB _____

4. a 4LC means GL _____

5. 52 C in a D of C _____

6. 4Q in a D _____

7. 3 sides on a T, but 4 sides on a S _____

8. 7 C on the planet E _____

9. an I has 6 L, but a S has 8 L _____

10. at 32 D, water F _____

11. GW was the first U.S. P _____

12. 360 D in a C _____

13. 64 S on a CB _____

14. 4 S on a V, but 6 S on a G _____

15. a U has 1 W, but a B has 2 W _____

Riddles

Answer Key

Page 198

1. scatterbrained
2. backwards glance
3. square meal
4. neon light
5. little league
6. big man on campus
7. pain in the neck
8. sleeping on the job
9. long time, no see
10. age before beauty
11. double date
12. high school

Page 199

1. what goes up must come down
2. banana split
3. talking in his sleep
4. one in a million
5. eggs over easy
6. three-ring circus
7. go for it
8. no two ways about it
9. good over evil
10. one on one
11. slow down
12. stand in a corner

Page 200

1. mirror
2. the appearance of the letter e
3. on a map
4. as much wood as a woodchuck could chuck if a woodchuck could chuck wood
5. breakfast and lunch
6. 3, because half of 2 = 1, and then 1 + 2 = 3
7. 12 (January 2nd, February 2nd, etc.)
8. He makes the faces of clocks/watches.
9. 1:12, or 12 after 1
10. a shoe

Page 201

1. carpet
2. fire
3. a cold
4. a nose
5. a mushroom
6. corn
7. a stamp
8. a towel
9. darkness
10. stars

Page 202

1. 26 letters in the alphabet
2. 52 weeks in a year
3. Thomas Edison invented the light bulb
4. a four-leaf clover means good luck
5. 52 cards in a deck of cards
6. four quarters in a dollar
7. three sides on a triangle, but four sides on a square
8. seven continents on the planet Earth
9. an insect has six legs, but a spider has eight legs
10. at 32 degrees, water freezes
11. George Washington was the first U.S. president
12. 360 degrees in a circle
13. 64 squares on a chess board
14. four strings on a violin, but six strings on a guitar
15. a unicycle has one wheel, but a bicycle has two wheels

Licensed to Work

A car's license plate can tell something about its owner. Decode these plates to reveal clues about the what kind of work the car's owner does. Choose the name of a job from the box below and write it on the line under the appropriate license plate.

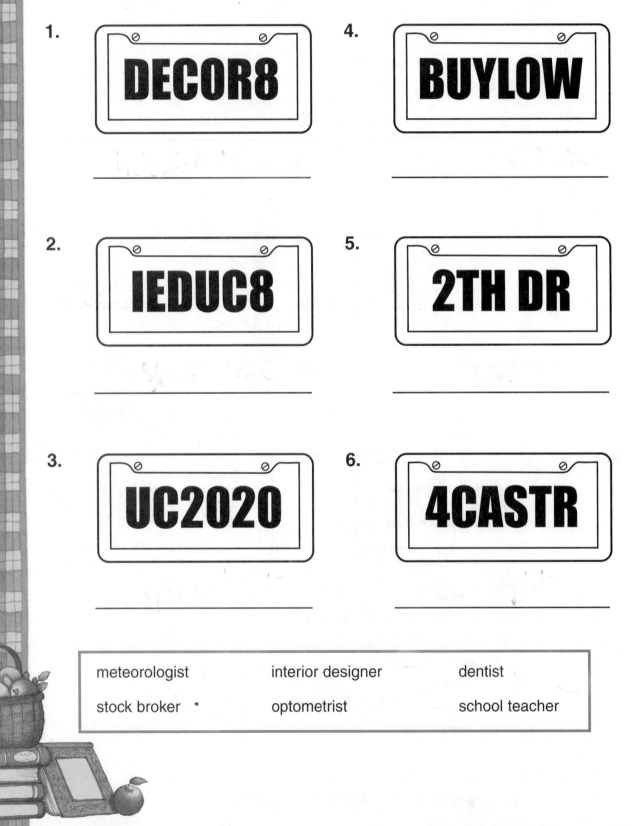

1. DECOR8

_____

4. BUYLOW

_____

2. IEDUC8

_____

5. 2TH DR

_____

3. UC2020

_____

6. 4CASTR

_____

meteorologist	interior designer	dentist
stock broker	optometrist	school teacher

Licensed to Work (cont.)

A car's license plate can tell something about its owner. Decode these plates to reveal clues about the what kind of work the car's owner does. Choose the name of a job from the box below and write it on the line under the appropriate license plate.

1. **LOCKMUP**

   _____

4. **ISU M4U**

   _____

2. **I OPER8**

   _____

5. **SLM DNK**

   _____

3. **UXRSIZE**

   _____

6. **DO ULIE**

   _____

surgeon ✓	lawyer ✓	law enforcement ✓
personal trainer	polygraph tester	basketball player

Initials

Use only one or two letters of the alphabet to answer these questions.

1. an insect that stings

   _____

2. a large body of water

   _____

3. a question you could ask

   _____

4. a female sheep

   _____

5. opposite of full

   _____

6. number before 81

   _____

7. not difficult

   _____

8. jealousy

   _____

9. alright

   _____

10. a green vegetable

    _____

11. a blue bird

    _____

12. a written composition

    _____

More Riddles

Answer Key

Page 204

1. interior designer
2. school teacher
3. optometrist
4. stock broker
5. dentist
6. meteorologist

Page 206

1. B (bee)
2. C (sea)
3. Y (Why?)
4. U (ewe)
5. MT (empty)
6. AT (eighty)
7. EZ (easy)
8. NV (envy)
9. OK (okay)
10. P (pea)
11. J (jay)
12. SA (essay)

Page 205

1. law enforcement
2. surgeon
3. personal trainer
4. lawyer
5. basketball player
6. polygraph tester

Scribble Art

Materials: paper, pencil, crayons or colored pencils

Directions: This is fun for everyone because you get to create a picture without even knowing it. Scribble on a piece of paper. Now stare at what you've done and look for a picture of something. It takes a lot of imagination to find a picture in a bunch of scribbles. Stare at what you've made. Look for some kind of shape to pop out at you. Try turning the page around to view it at different angles. View it from close up and far away. If you can't find anything after a couple of minutes, try adding some lines. If you still can't find anything, try a new scribble. This takes some practice. Once you find a creature, you can add whatever you need to finish the creature. Don't forget to give your creature a name.

What do you see? What will it be? Here is an example of scribble art:

Build a Mansion

Directions: Cut apart the puzzle pieces. Then, shuffle the pieces up and put them back together correctly to form the original picture.

Grid Drawing I

Use the blank grid below to draw your own seal.

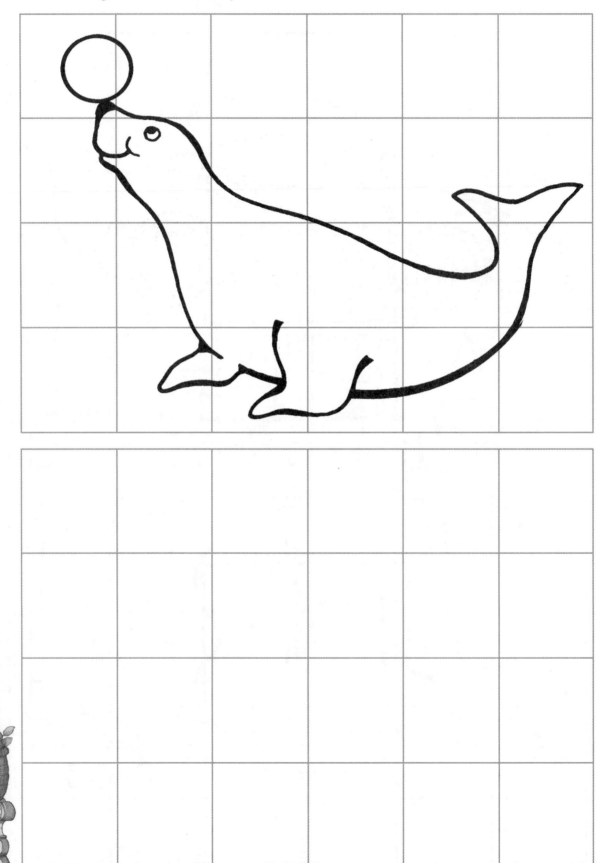

Grid Drawing II

Use the blank grid below to draw your own racecar.

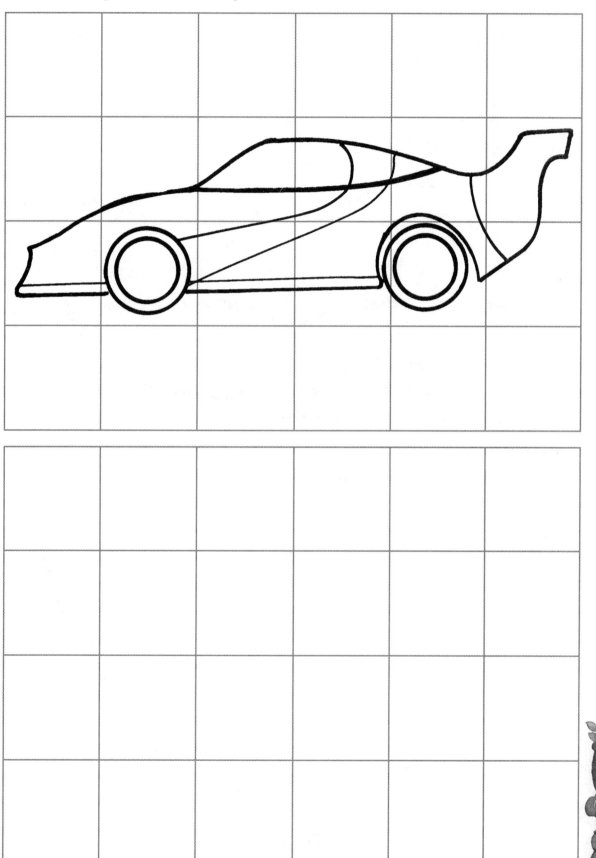

My Family Shield

Follow these directions to create your family shield:

❏ In box 1, draw a picture of the people in your family

❏ In box 2, draw a picture of something your family enjoys doing together.

❏ In box 3, draw a picture of some place you have traveled or visited with your family.

❏ In box 4, draw a picture of your house.

❏ In box 5, draw a picture of your pet or a pet you would like to have.

❏ In box 6, draw a picture of one of your favorite relatives (grandparent, aunt, uncle, cousin, etc.).

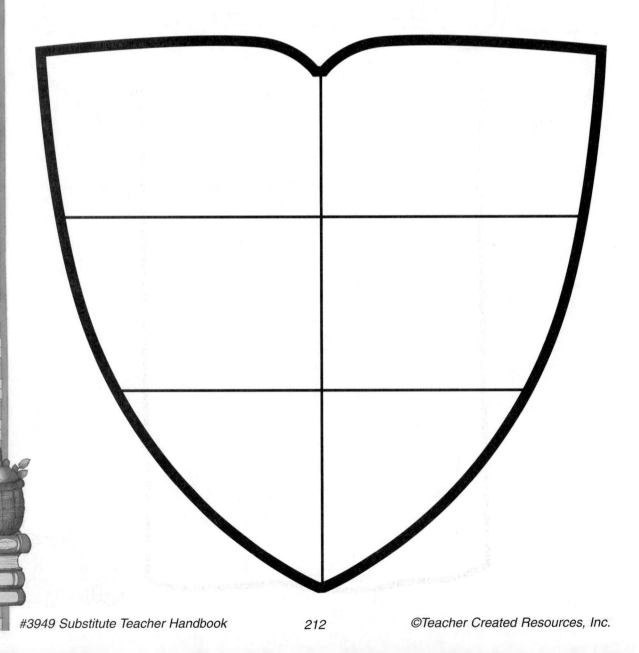

Design a T-Shirt

Directions: Start with a blank, white T-shirt, and then follow these directions to create an article of clothing that says something about you.

❑ Add your initials or nickname.

❑ Draw a picture that shows what you like to do. Use your favorite colors.

Name Art

Directions: This is one project that looks better and better only when you finally put the parts together. Have the students fold a 9" x 12" piece of construction paper in half lengthwise with the fold facing them. They write their name in pencil and cut around the letters. Make sure the letters connect so that when they cut it out it will stay together. Glue the names on a piece of butcher paper.

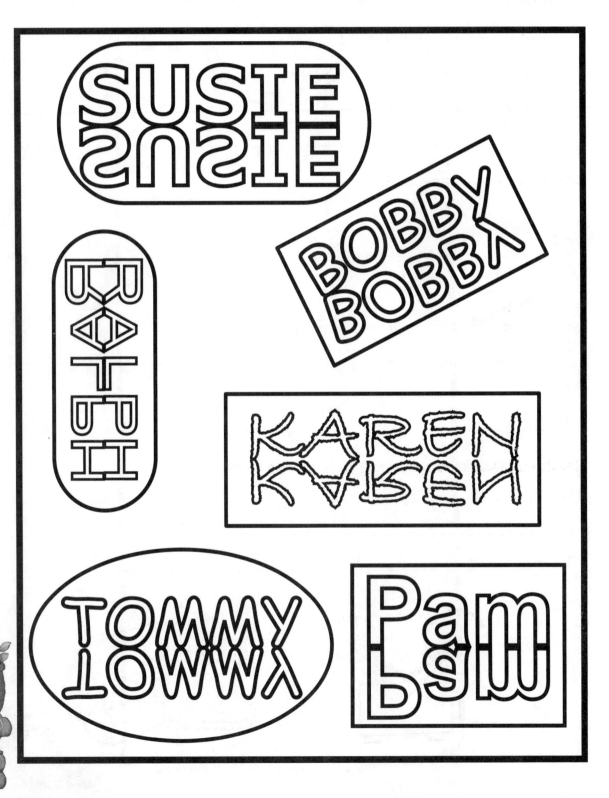

214

Video/Movie Log

Directions: To make this video more meaningful for you, please fill out the following information.

Video Title: _____

Describe the content of the video. _____

_____

_____

_____

List three main ideas mentioned in the video.

1. _____

2. _____

3. _____

List three things that you learned from the video.

1. _____

2. _____

3. _____

List three reasons to recommend this video to others.

1. _____

2. _____

3. _____

Guest Teacher Report

Substitute: _____   Date: _____

Phone Number: _____   Class: _____

My Phone Number: _____   Grade Level: _____

Today's lessons:

_____

_____

_____

_____

_____

_____

Additional things we covered:

_____

_____

Star students:

_____

_____

Absent students: _____

Notes for you: _____

_____

Your substitute teacher,

_____
(Signature)

Guest Teacher Report

Substitute: _____   Date: _____

Phone Number: _____   Class: _____

My Phone Number: _____   Grade Level: _____

Period	My Notes on the Lessons	Notes Concerning the Students
1		
2		
3		
4		
5		
6		
7		
8		

Your substitute teacher,

_____

(Signature)

Recommended Reading List

Books for Ages 5-6

Best, Cari. *Three Cheers for Catherine the Great!* Farrar, Straus and Giroux, 2003.

Brett, Jan. *Town Mouse, Country Mouse.* Putnam Juvenile, 2002.

Chall, Marsha Wilson. *Bonaparte.* Dorling Kindersley Publishing, 2000.

Danziger, Paula. *It's Justin Time, Amber Brown.* Putnam Juvenile, 2001.

Darrow, Sharon. *Old Thunder and Miss Raney.* DK Publishing, Inc., 2000.

Freeman, Don. *Corduroy at the Zoo.* Viking, 2001.

Gonzalez, Lucia M. *The Bossy Gallito.* Sagebrush Education Resources, 1999.

Henkes, Kevin. *Chrysanthemum.* William Morrow & Company, Inc., 1996.

Hutchins, Pat. *The Doorbell Rang.* William Morrow & Company, Inc., 1989.

McCloskey, Robert. *Make Way for Ducklings.* Puffin, 1998.

Milne, A.A. *Winnie the Pooh.* Puffin, 1992.

Piper, Watty. *The Little Engine that Could.* Grosset & Dunlap, 2001.

Potter, Beatrix. *The Tale of Peter Rabbit.* Penguin Putnam Books for Young Readers, 2004.

Samuels, Barbara. *Aloha, Dolores.* DK Publishing, Inc., 2000.

Schwartz, Amy. *How to Catch an Elephant.* DK Publishing, Inc., 2001.

Sendak, Maurice. *Where the Wild Things Are.* HarperCollins Children's Books, 1984.

Shannon, George. *Tomorrow's Alphabet.* William Morrow & Company, Inc., 1999.

Steig, William. *Amos and Boris.* Farrar, Straus and Giroux, 1977.

Suen, Anastasia. *Hamster Chase.* Puffin, 2002.

Viorst, Judith. *Alexander and the Terrible, Horrible, No Good, Very Bad Day.* Simon & Schuster Children's, 1976.

Wood, Audrey. *Quick as a Cricket.* Child's Play-International, 1991.

Yolen, Jane. *Owl Moon.* Philomel, 1987.

Books for Ages 7-8

Best, Cari. *Three Cheers for Catherine the Great!* Farrar, Straus and Giroux, 2003.

Blume, Judy. *Freckle Juice.* Bantam Doubleday Dell Books for Young Readers, 1978.

Danziger, Paula. *It's Justin Time, Amber Brown.* Putnam Juvenile, 2001.

Darrow, Sharon. *Old Thunder and Miss Raney.* DK Publishing, Inc., 2000.

dePaola, Tomie. *The Art Lesson.* Putnam Juvenile, 1997.

DeFelice, Cynthia C. *Cold Feet.* DK Publishing, Inc., 2000.

Freeman, Don. *Corduroy at the Zoo.* Viking, 2001.

Kajikawa, Kimiko. *Yoshi's Feast.* DK Publishing, Inc., 2000.

Lester, Helen. *Author: A True Story.* Houghton Mifflin Company, 2002.

Lionni, Leo. *Swimmy.* Alfred A. Knopf, Inc., 1973.

Nixon, Joan Lowery. *If You Were a Writer.* Simon & Schuster Children's, 1995.

Noble, Trinka. *The Day Jimmy's Boa Ate the Wash.* Puffin, 1984.

Plecas, Jennifer. *Agapanthus Hum and Major Bark.* Philomel, 2001.

Prelutsky, Jack. *The New Kid on the Block.* Greenwillow Books, 1990.

Samuels, Barbara. *Aloha, Dolores.* DK Publishing, Inc., 2000.

Schwartz, Amy. *How to Catch an Elephant.* DK Publishing, Inc., 2001.

Recommended Reading List (cont.)

Books for Ages 7-8 (cont.)

Suen, Anastasia. *Hamster Chase*. Puffin, 2002.

——. *Willie's Birthday*. Puffin, 2002.

Williams, Vera B. *A Chair for My Mother*. William Morrow & Company, Inc., 1984.

Woodson, Jacqueline. *The Other Side*. Putnam Juvenile, 2001.

Books for Ages 9-10

Atwater, Richard and Florence. *Mr. Popper's Penguins*. Little, Brown & Company, 1992.

Blume, Judy. *Tales of a Fourth Grade Nothing*. Puffin, 2003.

Cleary, Beverly. *Dear Mr. Henshaw*. HarperCollins Publishers, 1994.

Dahl, Roald. *James and the Giant Peach*. Puffin, 1996.

Fitzhugh, Louise. *Harriet the Spy*. Bantam Doubleday Dell Books for Young Readers, 2001.

MacLachlan, Patricia. *Sarah, Plain and Tall*. HarperCollins Children's Books, 1987.

Naylor, Phyllis Reynolds. *Shiloh*. Simon & Schuster Children's, 2000.

Silverstein, Shel. *Where the Sidewalk Ends*. Dell Publishing Company, Inc., 1986.

White, E.B. *Stuart Little*. HarperCollins Publishers, 1974.

Books for Younger Teens

Babbitt, Natalie. *Tuck Everlasting*. Farrar, Straus and Giroux, 2000.

Burnett, Frances Hodgson. *The Secret Garden*. HarperCollins Children's Books, 1987.

Creech, Sharon. *Walk Two Moons*. HarperCollins Children's Books, 1996.

Dahl, Roald. *The BFG*. Puffin, 1998.

Gardiner, John Reynolds. *Stone Fox*. HarperCollins Children's Books, 1983.

Hesse, Karen. *Out of the Dust*. Scholastic, Inc., 1998.

L'Engle, Madeleine. *A Wrinkle in Time*. Scholastic, Inc., 2003.

MacLachlan, Patricia. *Sarah, Plain and Tall*. HarperCollins Children's Books, 1987.

Naylor, Phyllis Reynolds. *Shiloh*. Simon & Schuster Children's, 2000.

O'Brien, Robert C. *Mrs. Frisby and the Rats of NIMH*. Aladdin Paperbacks, 1975.

O'Dell, Scott. *Island of the Blue Dolphins*. Bantam Doubleday Dell Books for Young Readers, 1971.

Paterson, Katherine. *Bridge to Terabithia*. HarperCollins Children's Books, 2004.

Paulsen, Gary. *Hatchet*. Simon & Schuster Children's, 1999.

Silverstein, Shel. *Where the Sidewalk Ends*. Dell Publishing Company, Inc., 1986.

Taylor, Mildred D. *Roll of Thunder, Hear My Cry*. Puffin, 1997.

Wilder, Laura Ingalls. *Little House on the Prairie*. HarperCollins Children's Books, 1976.

Useful Books for Substitute Teachers

Below are books concerning substitute teaching. Some of the books are self-help, while others are about the experience of substitute teaching.

Cawthrone, Barbara. *Instant Success for Classroom Teachers, New and Substitute Teachers.* Greenfield Publications, 1981.

Collins, S. Harold. *Classroom Management for Substitute Teachers.* Garlic Press, 1982.

————. *Mastering the Art of Substitute Teaching.* Garlic Press, 1995.

————. *Substitute Ingredients.* Garlic Press, 100 Hillview Lane, #2, Eugene, OR 97401.

Dodd, Anne Wescott. *A Handbook for Substitute Teachers.* Charles C. Thomas Pub Ltd., 1989.

Manera, Elizabeth, Marji Gold-Vukson, and Jennifer Kapp. *Substitute Teaching: Planning for Success.* Kappa Delta Pi Publications, 1996.

Promin, Barbara. *Substitute Teaching: A Book for Hassle Free Substituting.* St. Martin's Press, 1983.

Redwine, Mary Frances. *Substitute Teacher's Handbook.* McGraw-Hill Children's Publishing, 1990.

Seeman, Cary and Shannon Hofstrand. *Super Sub: A Must-Have Handbook for Substitute Teachers.* Good Year Books, 1998.

Smith, Geoffrey, G. *Substitute Teacher Handbook (K–12).* Substitute Teacher Training Inst., 2002.

Wong, Harry K. and Rosemary Tripi. *The First Days of School: How to Be an Effective Teacher.* Harry K. Wong Publications, 1998.

220

Internet Search Keywords

Often substitute teachers need Internet resources to help out with upcoming lessons. Included are some wonderful search words and terms to help you find exactly what you need.

Mathematics

SCORE Online Mathematics Lessons

SCORE Additional Resources

SCORE Numbers in Search of a Problem

Math Forum

Mathematics Lesson Plans

K–12 Lessons and Curriculum Resource

Sylvan Math Lessons

Math Lesson Database

Free K–12 Math Activities

Yahoo! Directory Mathematics

Math Worksheets

Math Study Hall

General Math

Arithmetic Lesson Plans

Online Student Math Activities

Math Worksheets

Geometry Lesson Plans

Currency Lesson Plans

Language Arts

SCORE Literature K–8

SCORE Literature 9–12

CyberGuides: Teacher Guides and Student Activities

English Language Teaching/ Lesson Plans

English Language & ESL/ EFL Lesson Plans

Primary Games

Language Arts Printables

Reading Arts Printables

Reading/Language Arts Center

School Bell: Language Arts

Literature & Language Arts

The Write Site

Phonics, Reading, Writing, Spelling, Vocabulary

Book Series

Language Arts Lesson Plans

Awesome Library

AskERIC Language Arts Lesson Plans

Internet Search Keywords (cont.)

History/Social Science

SCORE History-Social Science Resources

SCORE History/Social Science Search Theme/Topic Biographies

Literature List Guide

Teacher Resources

Discovery Online Curriculum

Lesson Planning Center

Online Student Activities

Geography Printables

Map Library

Geography Challenge

Daily Almanac

Science

SCORE Science Lesson Plans

Whelmers

Lessons by Subject and Grade Level

Teacher Developed Lesson Plans

Massachusetts Lesson Plans

Effective Lesson Plans

Hands-on Science Ideas

Center for Science Education

Science Education Clearinghouse

Michigan Teacher Network

Interdisciplinary Studies in Science

LACOE K–12 Lesson Plans

Pattern Detectives

Science Schools Online

Physical Education

Physical Education Elementary Lesson Plans

Physical Education Middle School Lesson Plans

Physical Education High School Lesson Plans

Physical Education Resources

Physical Education Lesson Plans

Fitness

Heath Subject Area

Reach Every Child

Health and Physical Education Lesson Plans

Sports Media Lesson Plans

Instructional Materials in Physical Education

Physical Education Materials Search

Health, Nutrition, and P.E. Lesson Plans

Physical Education Instructional Resources

Internet Search Keywords (cont.)

Miscellaneous Lesson Plans

AskEric Lesson Plans

Busy Teachers' WebSite K–12

Blue Web Learning Site Library

Teachers.net Lessons

Internet Connections/Lesson Plans and
  Activities

Internet Lesson Plans

In the Classroom Lesson Plans on
  the Internet

WebQuest

Teachnet.com: Lesson Ideas

Lesson Exchange

TEAMS Distance Learning

Guide for Educators—Lesson Plans
  and Thinking Skills

Lesson Plans—Discovery Channel School

Encarta Lesson Collection

Free Lesson Plans

Free K–8 Lesson Plans

Free Classroom Activities

K–8 Web Sites

Sites for Teachers

Family Education

Integrating Technology Into Your Classroom

Worksheet Library

Quiz Library

Online Games

Online Quizzes

Online Projects

Educational Research

Notes from Research

AskEric

Classroom Discipline

New Teacher Page

Educators Reference Desk

Educational Research

Issues in Educational Research

Miscellaneous Educational Sites

Scholastic

The School Page: The Educator's
  Resources

Knowledge Adventure Home Page

The Global Schoolhouse

Great Substitute Resources

Puzzlemaker

Kids on the Web

Maps

Web Projects and Activities
  for Classroom Use

Sites for Teachers

About Education

Yahoo! Directory Education

U.S. Geological
  Survey Sites

Assignment Log

Date	School	Assignment Teacher/Class	Notes

224